PEOPLE STUDYING PEOPLE

PEOPLE STUDYING PEOPLE

Artifacts and Ethics in Behavioral Research

Ralph L. Rosnow

Temple University

Robert Rosenthal

Harvard University

W. H. FREEMAN AND COMPANY
NEW YORK

ACQUISITIONS EDITOR: Susan Finnemore Brennan
PROJECT EDITOR: Christine Hastings
COVER AND TEXT DESIGNER: Victoria Tomaselli
ILLUSTRATION COORDINATOR: Bill Page
PRODUCTION COORDINATOR: Maura Studley
COMPOSITION: W. H. Freeman Electronic Publishing Center/Susan Cory
MANUFACTURING: R R Donnelley & Sons Company

Library of Congress Cataloging-in-Publication Data

Rosnow, Ralph L.
    People studying people: artifacts and ethics in behavioral research/
    Ralph L. Rosnow, Robert Rosenthal.
        p.   cm.
    Includes bibliographical references and indexes.
    ISBN 0–7167–3070–7.   —ISBN 0–7167–3071–5 (pbk.)
    1. Psychology—Research.   2. Social sciences—Research.
  I. Rosenthal, Robert, 1933–   II. Title
  BF76.5.R645   1997
  150′.7′2—dc21   96–48978
                                                     CIP

Printed in the United States of America

First printing, 1997

We are as sailors who are forced to rebuild their ship on the open sea, without ever being able to start fresh from the bottom up. Wherever a beam is taken away, immediately a new one must take its place, and while this is done, the rest of the ship is used as support. In this way, the ship may be completely rebuilt like new with the help of the old beams and driftwood—but only through gradual rebuilding.[1]

—Otto Neurath

Contents

Preface

As noted in Otto Neurath's epigraph, it's never finished, the ship of science. And just as the old beams must constantly be replaced by the new, so must the old sailors be replaced by the new. These new sailors must learn from the old what factors weaken the beams and how beams are replaced. Artifacts in behavioral research are beam-weakening, and each successive generation of sailors must learn to spot these beam-weakeners. In this way, they keep improving the ship as it is conceptualized in Neurath's beautiful simile.

Replacing beams is essential, but it can also be dangerous. Passengers can be hurt during the improvement of the ship, and sailors must learn how to sail safely, harming no one aboard. Knowing about artifacts and their control helps keep the ship seaworthy; knowing about research ethics keeps the sailors worthy and the passengers safe.

The main purpose of this book is to pass along to the young sailors an overview of what is known about artifacts and ethics in behavioral research. To accomplish this, we draw on the literature of the last 100 years of our science, with an emphasis on the golden age of artifactology. We owe a great deal to the early artifactologists and ethicists of behavioral research, from the paleopioneers, including Oskar Pfungst and Saul Rosenzweig, to the early pioneers, including John Adair, Henry Beecher, Edwin Boring, Donald Campbell, Lee Cronbach, Herbert Hyman, John Jung, Jay Katz, Herbert Kelman, Robert Lana, William

McGuire, Martin Orne, Henry Riecken, Milton Rosenberg, and Irwin Silverman. Although most of our illustrations focus on behavioral research, Neurath's simile implies that the concern with artifacts is not restricted to behavioral or social science. Thus we also note examples from physics, biology, and other scientific areas, as well as cases from outside science that imply a common thread in the nature of knowledge and the endeavor to make sense of the world.

Our own work presented here originally appeared in various journal articles or in a number of books and chapters that are no longer in print; readers who are interested in a more detailed or more technical discussion will find citations of each of the particular sources in this book. We are grateful to a long list of coworkers--including many brilliant graduate students--with whom we have been fortunate to collaborate, beginning at Boston University and the University of North Dakota and continuing at Temple University and Harvard University. We would like to acknowledge the support that Rosnow received over the years from the National Science Foundation and Temple University's Thaddeus L. Bolton Endowment, and the support that Rosenthal received over the years from the National Science Foundation, more recently from the Spencer Foundation, and currently from a James McKeen Cattell Sabbatical Award. We thank Susan Brennan of W. H. Freeman and Company for her enthusiasm for this project, and we thank the following reviewers for their helpful comments and suggestions: Steven M. Specht, Lebanon Valley College; Susan E. Dutch, Westfield State College; Catherine S. Murray, St. Joseph's University; Elizabeth L. Paul, Trenton State College; David Kenny, University of Connecticut; George S. Rotter, Montclair State; and Roxane Cohen Silver, University of California-Irvine. We thank Margaret Ritchie for once again improving our writing, and we thank Mimi Rosnow and Mary Lu Rosenthal for improving us in ways too numerous to mention.

This is our 11th book together in a collaboration that began over 30 years ago, and the beat goes on!

PEOPLE STUDYING PEOPLE

Chapter 1

Artifacts in Behavioral Research

All scientific inquiry is subject to error, and it is far better to be aware of this, to study the sources in an attempt to reduce it, and to estimate the magnitude of such errors in our findings, than to be ignorant of the errors concealed in the data. One must not equate ignorance of error with the lack of error. The lack of demonstration of error in certain fields of inquiry often derives from the nonexistence of methodological research into the problem and merely denotes a less advanced stage of that profession.

—Herbert Hyman[1]

The Nature of Artifacts

The effort to understand human behavior must itself be one of the oldest of human behaviors. But for all the centuries of effort, there is much we do not yet know. The unsolved behavioral problems of mental illness, racism, sexism, and violence, both the idiosyncratic and institutionalized, bear witness to how much we do not yet know. Because of the urgency of the questions waiting to be answered, it should not be surprising that behavioral scientists, and the publics that support them, suffer from a certain impatience. That impatience is understandable, but perhaps, from time to time, we need to remind ourselves that Neurath's "ship of science" has not been afloat very long in the behavioral sciences.

The application of that reasoning and of those procedures that we call the *scientific method* to the understanding of human behavior is of relatively recent origin. Yet what we have learned about human behavior in the short period, say, from Wilhelm Wundt's founding of experimental psychology in Leipzig in 1879 until now is out of all proportion to what was learned in the preceding centuries. Although most of what we want to know is still unknown, this success of the application of "scientific method" to the study of human behavior has given us great hope of an accelerating return of knowledge on our investment of time and effort. To be sure, this application of what we think of as scientific method has not simplified human behavior; instead, it has shown us more clearly just how complex human behavior really is.

In modern behavioral science, the research participant (or "research subject") serves as our model of people in general, or at least of a certain kind of person. We know that behavior is complex because we sometimes change this person's world ever so slightly and detect substantial changes in his or her behavior, while at other times we change that world greatly and detect hardly any changes in behavior. It is as if the research participants' minds were somehow in a different world from ours. We also know that behavior is complex because a careful experiment conducted in one place at one time often yields results very different from the "same" experiment conducted in another place at another time. We have learned that much of the complexity of human behavior is inherent, but we have also learned that some of this complexity may result from uncontrolled aspects of the research situation, especially from the interaction between the researcher and the participant.

We can conceptualize this portion of the complexity of behavior, which can be attributed to the intrinsic human aspects of behavioral and social research, as a set of *artifacts* (or systematic errors) to be isolated, measured, considered, and, sometimes, eliminated. That is, artifacts are not simply inconsequential effects in a research design; they may actually jeopardize the validity of the researcher's inferences from his or her results. Another way of saying this is that artifacts are unintended or uncontrolled human aspects of the research situation that confound the investigator's conclusions about what went on in the study. As we shall see later, artifacts can also teach us about topics of substantive interest. Indeed, as William McGuire observed, today's artifact may be tomorrow's independent variable;[2] that is, the same conditions discounted as "nuisance variables" at one time may later be exploited as variables of interest in their own right.

Clever Hans

The systematic investigation of artifacts began in the late 1950s, the bulk of the research following in the 1960s and 1970s. Well before this work began in earnest, there had been early indications that artifacts might be lurking in the investigative procedures used by behavioral scientists. A classic case showed that artifacts could result from the observer's expectations or hypotheses. In this 1904 case, a German psychologist, Oscar Pfungst, carried out a six-week investigation of a remarkable horse owned by a mathematics teacher named Wilhelm von Osten.[3] Since the beginning of recorded civilization, there had been reports of "learned animals," but no animal had so captured the imagination of the general public and of European psychology as von Osten's horse, "Clever Hans." Pfungst's elegant series of studies solved the riddle of Hans's amazing performance and implied how easily observers can be deceived by the self-fulfilling nature of their expectations.

Before Pfungst had entered the scene, rumors had circulated widely of the astounding "intellectual" feats performed by Hans. By tapping his hoof according to a code taught to him by von Osten, Hans was said to answer questions put to him in German. Asked to spell a word, Hans would tap out the letters, aided ostensibly by a code table set in front of him. To respond yes to a question, he would nod his head up and down; to respond no, he would execute a deliberate sideways motion. Asked by an observer how much 2/5 plus 1/2 is, Hans would tap first 9 and then 10 for 9/10. Hans was also rumored to possess an excellent memory: He knew the value of all the German coins. He knew the entire yearly calendar and could name the day of the week of any date mentioned. He could tell the time to the minute. If a sentence were pronounced for him only once, he could repeat the entire sentence the following day. He recognized people after having seen them once, even from photographs taken of them in previous years or from pictures that bore only a slight resemblance.

Unlike the owners of other clever animals of that period, von Osten did not profit financially from his horse's talents. Thus it seemed unlikely that von Osten had any fraudulent intent, and in fact, he was quite willing to let others, even in his absence, question Hans. Intentional cues from von Osten could thus be ruled out as the reason for the horse's abilities. But in a series of experiments, Pfungst identified three conditions that, when varied, moderated the horse's cleverness. First, when Hans was fitted with blinders so that he could not see his questioners, his accuracy immediately dropped off. Second, as the distance between Hans and his questioners was increased, his accuracy diminished. From these findings, Pfungst concluded that Hans was "clever" only when he was in visual proximity to his questioners. Third, the horse's accuracy also diminished when the questioner did not know the answer. Hans's performance was evidently due to something other than his capacity to reason.

Pfungst discovered that Hans responded to very subtle cues given to him by his questioners, not just intentional cues, but unwitting movements and mannerisms. Someone would ask Hans a question requiring a long tapping response, and the person might then lean forward as though settling down for a long wait. Hans responded to the questioner's forward movement, not to the actual question, and kept tapping away with his hoof until the questioner communicated his expectancy that Hans would stop tapping. This the questioner might do by suddenly straightening up in anticipation that Hans was about to reach the correct number of taps. Hans was sensitive to even more subtle cues: the raising of an eyebrow or the dilation of nostrils. Pfungst demonstrated that anyone could start Hans tapping and then stop his tapping by the use of such cues. What was of particular interest to Pfungst was that Hans often received quite unintended cues from his questioners, even from Pfungst himself.

Pfungst's studies provided an object lesson in the susceptibility of behavior (even animal behavior) to unconscious suggestion. If a horse's behavior could be affected simply by an observer's expectations, might a human research participant be similarly affected by the expectations and hypotheses of an experimenter? A half century would pass before this plausible artifact was reliably demonstrated. In the meantime, another important development fostered the suspicion that research participants behaved in special ways *because* they knew they were "subjects" of investigation. This principle, called the *Hawthorne effect*,[4] grew out of a series of human factors experiments meant to examine the effects of working conditions on employees' performance.[5] It would ultimately spawn an area of artifact investigation known as the *social psychology of the experiment.*

The Hawthorne Studies

Between 1924 and 1932, a group of industrial researchers conducted a series of field experiments at the Hawthorne works of the Western Electric Company in Cicero, Illinois, which manufactured equipment for the Bell Telephone Company. One set of studies examined the impact of higher levels of electric lighting, increased rest periods, and other conditions on the work productivity of young women who inspected parts, assembled relays, or wound coils.[6] According to news reports and a Western Electric memorandum, one study revealed that any improvement in working conditions resulted in greater worker satisfaction and increased productivity. When the improvements were removed, however, the productivity did not decline; the efficiency actually continued to increase, according to the reports. On interviewing the team of six workers who had participated in this particular study, the researchers concluded that their productivity increases had been driven by their feeling flattered by being subjects of investigation. That is, they had been motivated to increase their output because of their special status as research participants. Not only were their opinions being solicited by management, but they had been singled out for free morning tea, rest periods, and shorter hours of work.[7]

The original reports and secondary accounts of this study have been repeatedly subjected to critical analysis, and the critics have argued that the historical record was tainted by sweeping generalizations embroidered by overly zealous authors.[8] For example, in a fascinating piece of detective work, H. McIlvaine Parsons, a specialist in human factors research, believed that he had discovered a long-ignored confounding variable that explained the Hawthorne effect.[9] The assembly line workers had been told their output rates, and the higher the rates, the more they were paid, Parsons discovered. Putting the facts together, he argued that the increased productivity had been reinforced by the feedback the workers had received about their output rates. Like some projective test into which people read their own meanings, Parsons argued, the Hawthorne effect was a mixture of fantasy and reality into which textbook authors had read their own meaning.

Nevertheless, the principle of the Hawthorne effect entered into the vocabulary of behavioral science as implying a kind of "placebo effect" in psychological research.[10] A placebo is a treatment intended to have no effect (e.g., a fake pill used in a drug evaluation experiment); it is usually given to a control group to provide a comparison with the effects of the drug (the real pill) given to an experimental group. Because merely being given a pill that *may* be real can produce an effect, the purpose of this design is to separate this placebo effect from the effect of taking the drug. On the surface, such an experiment seems simple enough, but once we look deeper, we realize that "taking a drug" means something quite different from merely getting a chemical into the blood stream. Taking a drug means, among other things, (1) having someone give the participant the drug; (2) having someone give the participant the attention that goes with giving the drug; (3) having the participant believe that relevant medication has been administered; and (4) having the ingredients of the drug find their way into the blood system. The Hawthorne effect implied that many participants in psychology experiments responded not just to the experimental treatment, but also to uncontrolled factors, including the belief that they were being administered a treatment intended to have a particular effect. The direction and magnitude of the resulting artifacts were unclear. It was even unclear whether any artifacts were present at all.[11] Nonetheless, researchers were warned to be wary of unleashing a Hawthorne effect by their manipulations, observations, or measurements, a warning that was dutifully communicated to several generations of researchers even while the ship of behavioral science stood its steady course.

Rosenzweig's Critique

In 1933, another conceptual advance in the social psychology of the experiment was made by a clinical psychologist fresh out of graduate school, Saul Rosenzweig. He published an insightful critique in which he examined different aspects of the psychology experiment, proceeding on the assumption that "when one

8

works with human materials one must reckon with the fact that everyone is a psychologist." He continued:

> How many subjects in a psychological experiment are purely receptive? How many are willing fully to adopt the humble role of subject in an investigation of their motives, aims and thoughts? Most, as a matter of fact, are carrying on a train of psychological activity that is rather about the experiment than a part of it by intention of the [experimenter]. "Where did I see that man before?—What is he getting at anyhow?—I wonder if he will ask me about this?—I won't tell him about that.—Could H. have been here for the same test?—How stupid that experimenter looks!—What a loud necktie!—How stupid he must think I am!—When will this be over?"[12]

Rosenzweig identified three distinct sources of systematic errors in the psychology experiment. First, errors might result from the "observational attitude" of the experimenter. Rosenzweig described how chemists take into account the ambient temperature, possibly even the heat of their own body; experimenting psychologists, he urged, should take into account their attitudes toward their research participants and the participants' beliefs about and attitudes toward the experiment.

Second, when Rosenzweig said, "Everyone is a psychologist," he was alluding to "errors of motivational attitude." Chemists work with inanimate materials, but in psychology, the "materials" carry on a train of thought in which they try to guess the purpose of the study and to anticipate how the experimenter will evaluate them. The experimenter, Rosenzweig stated, is often unaware of the insidious ways in which the "motivational attitude" may creep into an experiment and bias the results.

Third, according to Rosenzweig, there are "errors of personality influence." These emanate from such factors as the experimenter's warmth or coolness, unguarded gestures or words of the experimenter, and the experimenter's sex and race. Any of these factors may affect the attitudes and reactions of research participants, quite apart from the experimental manipulation. Rosenzweig sketched some procedures that he thought might help to obviate these "errors," including "simple deceptions" to prevent errors of motivational attitude. He cautioned, however, that it is often unclear whether the experimenter or the participant is the "true deceiver." This warning would be repeated in the 1960s by other writers.[13]

Resistance to the Artifact Idea

Previously, we alluded to McGuire's theory of the distinct stages in the life of artifacts. At first, people seemed unaware of artifacts and denied their existence even when they were pointed out. Once researchers perceived artifacts as nuisance variables, they looked for ways to eliminate or control them.[14] In the third stage, McGuire argued, artifacts began to be exploited as independent variables of substantive interest in their own right. The philosopher Arthur Schopenhauer also spoke of three stages through which every truth seems to pass: ridicule, opposition, and recognition as self-evident. It took a long time for many influential psychologists to concede the presence of the "errors" identified by Rosenzweig, much less recognize their existence as self-evident. Given the porosity of memory, it is a story that bears repeating to each generation of young researchers[15] so that they do not, as Hyman warned, equate "ignorance of error with the lack of error."[16]

Several reasons have been suggested for the many years it took the existence of artifacts to be fully absorbed into the mainstream of behavioral methodology. One plausible reason is that artifacts presupposed the active influence of conscious cognitions.[17] The great chemist Antoine Lavoisier said that "the human mind gets creased into a way of seeing things," and the minds of many influential psychologists were creased in a way that perceived "consciousness" as not belonging within the domain of behavioral science. John B. Watson, who founded behaviorism, had urged fellow researchers to "discard all references to consciousness"[18] and to develop "a purely objective experimental branch of natural science."[19] By emphasizing only observable responses as acceptable data, Watsonian behaviorists essentially dismissed anything having to do with cognition as a variable of less than scientific relevance.[20]

Another plausible reason for the resistance to acknowledging artifacts was concern that an admission of the systematic errors that are part and parcel of research with human participants would impede the growing influence of our science. After World War II, there was a tremendous growth in psychology departments and an increased role for research psychologists in the government, the military, and industry as a result of optimism about the likely benefits of behavioral science. Many people believed that, as social psychologist Irwin Silverman put it, psychology's identity crisis was over.[21] Critics who voiced concerns about artifacts were seen as undermining the empirical foundation of the scientific facts and theories that were proliferating in behavioral research.

A third reason for the resistance was that certain remnants of positivistic ideals were rampant in psychological science. Auguste Comte, who coined the term *positivism* in the first half of the 19th century, insisted that principles of behavior be expressed as physicalistic propositions, along the lines of a kind of "social physics."[22] Early psychologists referred to their research participants as *reagents,* a term borrowed from chemistry.[23] A chemical reagent is a substance that, carefully mixed with another substance in a clean test tube, invariably produces a certain reaction. Yet it was evident that the "test tubes" (i.e., research settings) and "reagents" (research participants) of psychological researchers were "contaminated" by the needs, anxieties, self-deceptions, and intentions of human beings who knew very well that their behavior was being scrutinized as part of a scientific study.[24] The use of terms such as reagent and subject implied a biological, stimulus-response machine. The term *participant* implies a "free, intentional" agent,[25] susceptible to external pressures but able to evaluate them and act independently on the basis of personal needs and objectives.

Random Versus Systematic Error

Previously, we alluded to artifacts as systematic errors—as opposed to random errors. In everyday usage, *systematic* implies a specific pattern of arrangement, whereas *random* usually implies a haphazard arrangement. To understand the technical difference between the two types of error (random and systematic), we can think of a grocer who weighs a bunch of grapes a number of times in a row. In an ideal world, his measurements would give the same result every time he (or somebody else) weighed the same bunch of grapes. In reality, his measurements, no matter how precise, will always come out a bit differently. Some of his measurements will slightly overestimate the true weight of the grapes, and other measurements will slightly underestimate the true weight. The problem is to estimate the true weight, which we can easily do because these overestimates and underestimates are a reflection of random errors. By simply averaging the measurements, we assume that random errors in the overestimates and underestimates will cancel one another and that the average will be a pretty good estimate of the true weight of the grapes.

But suppose we had a grocer who always weighed grapes with a thumb on the scale (i.e., introducing a systematic error), thus always inflating the price of grapes by tacking extra ounces onto the true weight. Generally speaking, random errors can be said to push measurements up and down around an exact value, so that the average of all the measurements over many trials is very close to the exact value. Systematic error (also called bias), on the other hand, tends to push measurements in the same direction and causes the average value to be consistently too large or too small. Thus random errors are likely to cancel out, on the average, over many repeated measurements; systematic errors do not cancel out but affect (or bias) all measurements in roughly the same way. Artifacts, because they are a type of systematic error, operate like a grocer with his thumb on the scale.

To be sure, it is relatively rare that scientists actually try to distort the truth, but some illustrative cases will be noted later. More often, the systematic error is unintentional but, like the grocer's thumb on the scale, still pushes the conclusions in one direction. The problem faced by the artifactologists was to figure out the direction in which particular sources of systematic error might push the results. Knowing this, they could suggest ways for researchers to make more accurate assessments of their data and, sometimes, eliminate or circumvent the source of bias. How this problem was attacked is the topic of the rest of this book, in which we delve into the nature and control of artifacts, viewed from the perspective of the researcher (Chapters 2 and 3), the participants (Chapters 4 and 5), and the ethical imperatives that guide the efficient design and implementation of research studies (Chapter 6).

Chapter 2

Biasing Effects
of Investigators

*Elaborate apparatus plays an important part in the science of to-day,
but I sometimes wonder if we are not inclined to forget that the most
important instrument in research must always be the human mind.*

—W. I. B. Beveridge[1]

Interactional and Noninteractional Bias

Science is not a monolithic institution; indeed
there are a great many "ships of science." The
investigators who sail and reconstruct these ships include laboratory experimenters, survey researchers,
and field investigators of both the experimental and
nonexperimental kind. Whatever their method of
inquiry, all attempt to steer their ship of science on a
steady course in the pursuit of truth. As Beveridge's
statement reminds us, the pursuit of scientific truth
is not a mechanical but a very human (and thus a
subjective as well as an objective) process. Ultimately, it is through the minds and experiences of
individual investigators that our world is pried open

for scrutiny and understanding. If we hope to have dependable knowledge of the world, we must have dependable knowledge of the possible biases in the mind and conduct of the individual investigator.

This kind of knowledge is essential whenever we hope to learn something from empirical reasoning. The American philosopher Charles Sanders Peirce recognized that each of us carries the baggage of accepted wisdom. As a consequence, myth, folklore, and superstition sometimes greatly influence what we accept as new knowledge. Many people in earlier times thought they saw angels and witches, and there have been physicists in modern times who thought they saw "rays" (N rays, discussed later) which in actuality were mere figments of imagination and suggestibility. In the 15th century, when Copernicus explained to the Pope that the sun, not the earth, was the center of our universe, this revolutionary insight was rejected as totally antithetical to accepted wisdom. The advance of human understanding is strewn with similar cases, and science was developed to draw on empirical reasoning to help us resolve such cases of disagreement.

But scientists, like all humans, are susceptible to the biases imposed by human limitations of perception and cognition. In this chapter, we examine the potential biasing effects of scientists themselves, which we categorize as *noninteractional* or *interactional*. Noninteractional biases operate, so to speak, in the mind, in the eye, or in the hand of the scientist. In other words, they do not affect the responses of the research participants themselves. As defined in Table 2.1, three noninteractional artifacts are observer, interpreter, and intentional biases. On the other hand, the interactional kind of bias has a direct impact on the reactions of research participants. In this chapter, we discuss four such biases: biosocial, psychosocial, situational, and modeling effects. In the next chapter we concentrate on one additional interactional artifact: experimenter expectancy bias. This type of bias is reminiscent of how the questioners' wishful thinking became a self-fulfilling

Table 2.1

Researcher-Related Artifacts and Their Control

Noninteractional Artifacts

1. *Observer bias:* An overestimate or underestimate during the observation and recording phase; controlled by independent replication.

2. *Interpreter bias:* An error in the interpretation of data; controlled by access to data by other scientists.

3. *Intentional bias:* A fabrication or fraudulent manipulation of data; controlled by independent replication and by access to data by other scientists.

Interactional Artifacts

4. *Biosocial effect:* An error attributable to biosocial attributes of the researcher (e.g., sex, age, ethnicity, and race); controlled by independent replication, possibly with biosocial controls that identify the source of bias.

5. *Psychosocial effect:* An error attributable to psychosocial attributes of the researcher (e.g., personality); controlled by independent replication, possibly with psychosocial controls that identify the source of bias.

6. *Situational effect:* An error attributable to the nature of the research setting and the particular participants; controlled by independent replications across settings and participants.

7. *Modeling effect:* An error that is a function of the example set by the researcher; controlled by independent replications.

8. *Experimenter expectancy bias:* An error that results when the researcher's hypothesis leads unintentionally to behavior toward the participants that increases the likelihood that the hypothesis will be confirmed; discussed in Chapter 3.

---

prophecy in the Clever Hans case, but we will focus our attention on research and applications with human participants in psychology and education.

The Investigator as Observer

The human imagination powerfully affects beliefs and perceptions when wishful or fearful thinking takes hold. Edgar Morin, a sociologist, studied a frightening rumor that swept through the city of Orléans, France, in 1969.[2] It was rumored that young girls had been drugged and imprisoned by Jewish boutique proprietors and shipped to foreign centers of prostitution. It was further alleged that local Jews had bribed the police and government officials to remain silent. In fact, there was not a grain of truth to the story; no women had even been reported missing. Through his meticulous detective work, Morin discovered that people's imaginations had been triggered by a fictitious kidnapping plot that had been vividly reported in a popular French tabloid. Rumors spread when anxieties and uncertainties are rampant,[3] and these allegations fed on the anxieties and uncertainties nourished by deeply embedded bias.

In another case, Donald M. Johnson reported a scary event that, although perceived as real, existed only in the imagination of its alleged victims.[4] In September 1944, a number of women residents of Mattoon, Illinois, were purportedly assaulted by a "phantom anesthetist" who opened their bedroom windows while they slept and sprayed only them, and not their husbands, with a paralyzing gas. In an article in the *Journal of Abnormal and Social Psychology,* Johnson detailed the incident—which had drawn international attention to Mattoon—and concluded there was not a speck of truth in the allegation. The symptoms of the gasser's victims, Johnson surmised, resembled the classic psychiatric description of hysteria: nausea and vomiting, sudden and temporary paralysis of the limbs, palpitations, and dryness of the mouth and throat. There were never any physical traces of the prowler's presence, although the police acted quickly in each reported case. Moreover, the chemistry of the gas implied a contradictory nature: It would have had to be a potent, stable anesthetic with unusually rapid action, but it would also have had to be sufficiently unstable not to have the same toxic effect on someone else in the same bed. It had to be powerful enough to bring on paralysis and vomiting but could leave no observable traces. No such concoction existed outside science fiction or people's imagination, Johnson argued.

The common thread in these two cases is that experiences were distorted so that some fanciful event was then "observed" to exist. Scientists, despite their claims of objectivity, have sometimes been the victims of a similar phenomenon, in which wishful thinking leads to wishful seeing. A notorious case in the annals of physics was the "discovery" of so-called N rays by the French physicist André Blondlot in the early part of the 20th century. N rays, he contended, made reflected light more intense and were bent by aluminum; anyone could see this effect with the naked eye under proper conditions. In fact, there were many scientists who said they had seen Blondlot's N rays, though others reported difficulty trying to replicate his experiments.

How this episode unfolded was recounted in 1989 by Richard P. Feynman, who described how the physicist R. W. Wood "put an end to the N-ray."[5] Blondlot gave a public lecture and demonstration to show how N rays were bent by aluminum. He told the audience that he had constructed a sandwich of all kinds of lenses, with an aluminum prism in the middle. He then manipulated an apparatus that allegedly turned the prism slowly to show how N rays, in Feynman's description, "came up this way and bent that way."[6] All the while, Blondlot's assistant kept announcing the intensity of his readings for different angles. Blondlot told the audience it was necessary to darken the room because N rays were affected by light, and turning the light off would make the assistant's readings more sensitive. When the lights came back on at the end of the demonstration, there was Wood in the front row. He had surreptitiously taken the prism and was holding it high in the air, balanced on the tips of his fingers, for all to see![7] Here, for all *really* to see, was incontrovertible proof that N rays were nothing more than a figment of imagination.

All of us, of course, are susceptible to overstating or under-stating the occurrence of something because we think it exists in a particular way. As F. W. Lane put it, scientists, like all human beings, may unwittingly "equate what they *think* they see, and sometimes what they *want* to see, with what actually happens."[8] In an article entitled "Seeing's Believing," M. L. Johnson told of a radiologist who mistook a button caught in a patient's throat for a button "on the vest"—where a button *ought* to be present.[9] Johnson concluded, "Our assumptions define and limit what we see, i.e., we tend to see things in such a way that they will fit in with our assumptions even if this involves distortions or omission. We therefore may invert our title and say 'Believing Is Seeing.'"[10] One of us counted the recording errors in a small set of experiments that happened to be at hand. It was not a random sample of experiments, and we make no claims beyond the observations in this set. However, when there were detectable recording errors, they favored the researchers' hypotheses to a greater extent than would be expected by chance.[11]

Interpretation of Data

The interpretation of the data collected is another part of the research process that is subject to bias. A glance at any of the technical journals of contemporary psychology will suggest that, while investigators only rarely debate the observations made by one another, they often debate the interpretation of those observations. It is as difficult to state rules for the accurate interpretation of data as it is rules for the accurate observation of data, but the variety of interpretations offered to explain the same data imply that many of us must turn out to be wrong. The history of science generally and of psychology more specifically suggests that more of us are wrong longer than we need to be because we hold our theories not quite lightly enough.

Clinging to a theory does have its advantages, however. It keeps us motivated to make more crucial observations. In any case, interpreter biases seem less serious than observer biases because the former are public while the latter are private. Given a set of observations, their interpretation becomes generally available to the scientific community. We are free to agree or disagree with any specific interpretation, but this is not usually possible in the case of the observations themselves. Often these are made by a single investigator, so that we are not free to agree or disagree. We can only hope that no observer biases occurred, and we can (and should) repeat the observations if possible.

Examples of interpreter biases are not hard to come by in the physical, biological, and behavioral sciences.[12] In the physical sciences, there were Michelson and Morley's experiments on the speed of light, conducted in 1887. Their report showed that, whether the light signals were sent out in the direction of the earth's motion or not, the speed was the same. It is said that this counterintuitive result was the stimulus for Einstein's development of his theory of relativity in 1905, although Einstein himself denied the connection. The experiment by Michelson and Morley, however, was important to relativity theory and, in fact, had the result required by it. The results of these experiments were probably actually in error: There did appear to be an ether drift; and defined by a difference in the speed of light as a function of the signal's direction in relation to the earth's motion, this "ether drift" could have jeopardized relativity theory. That it did not illustrates an interpreter bias in physics.

Michael Polanyi[13] and Arthur Koestler[14] have given the details of this case. In 1902, some 15 years after the Michelson-Morley experiment, W. M. Hicks showed some ether drift in their original observations. Then, from 1902 to 1926, D. C. Miller repeated the classic experiment thousands of times and consistently obtained a drift of from 8 to 9 km per second. So well established was relativity theory by then, however, that Miller's work was largely discounted (even though he presented his complete evidence in 1925 to the American Physical Society, of which he was then president).

Still later, W. Kantor, using still more elegant instrumentation, demonstrated that the speed of light depended on the motion of the observer.

It is true, as Polanyi tells us, that there was other evidence from different workers of the absence of ether drift, as required by relativity theory. But that evidence was not available when Miller presented his data in 1925 nor during the many years before that when he had been making his observations. How do we decide whether there was a methodological artifact in Miller's work, so that people did well to discount it? Is there a possibility that some physicist, had she or he been taught to take apparently sound data seriously, might, because of these inconsistent data, have so modified relativity theory that it would be more powerful by far? Miller's data were ignored, but they were available to anyone to interpret.

An illustration of interpreter bias in psychology—in which the data were neither ignored or unavailable—was discussed by psychologists John J. Sherwood and Mark Nataupsky.[15] They were interested in whether biographical characteristics of individual psychologists might predict how they would interpret published data pertaining to racial differences in intelligence research. Sherwood and Nataupsky gathered biographical information from a large number of psychologists who had published comparative studies of the IQs of blacks and whites. Several biographical items (e.g., age, birth order, and education) were then examined for their possible influence on the nature-versus-nurture conclusions reached by these psychologists. The three theoretical alternatives used were (1) that the differences in IQ between blacks and whites are due to the innate inferiority of blacks; (2) that IQ differences are due to environmental factors; or (3) that no reliable differences in IQ exist. Sherwood and Nataupsky concluded that it was possible statistically to predict people's interpreter biases about this issue simply from their biographies.

Certain noninteractional artifacts are harder to classify as either observational or interpreter bias; instead, they fall in between. One example is how many researchers interpret "non-significant" p values as implying "no effect." When they say they "observed no difference," this observation may be based on a misinterpretation of what a significant or nonsignificant p value tells us. The p value is the probability of a Type I error in a test of significance (we have more to say about p values later); a "nonsignificant p" is sometimes merely a signal that the sample size (i.e., the number of participants in the study) was too small to allow the detection of the obtained effect at some preferred level of significance. The effect may be present, but it may end up buried in a Davy Jones's locker of data that perished for want of a more powerful statistical analysis. Simple statistical procedures that help us guard against mistaken interpretations require nothing more than a pocket calculator and the raw ingredients in published reports.[16] Using such procedures, we can decide for ourselves whether an interpretation of "no effect" or "no observed difference" was really warranted.

Intentional Error

An attitude that abhors dishonesty and that values integrity and honest scholarship is paramount in scientific practice. Unfortunately, the history of science tells us that deliberate falsification (e.g., rigged experiments or the presentation of faked results), although uncommon, does sometimes occur. It is called *intentional error* here. An example in geology some two centuries ago involved Johann Beringer's discovery of remarkable fossils, including Hebraic letters which he interpreted as "the elements of a second Divine book."[17] A short time after Beringer had published his findings and their important implications, another "fossil" turned up with his name inscribed on it! He had been taken in by someone else's deliberate falsification. Although he immediately tried to buy back copies of his book, the damage to his reputation had been done. The standard story was that Beringer's students had perpetrated the hoax. There is evidence, however, that the fraud was no schoolboy prank but two colleagues' (successful) effort to discredit him.[18] Here is a case where one scientist's interpreter bias could be attributed in large part to the intentional error of others.

The problem of both intentional and unintentional error in the behavioral sciences may not differ from the problem in the sciences generally. Nevertheless, it has been said that, at least in the physical sciences, either intentional or unintentional errors are quickly checked by replication. Human nature being what it is, replication in the behavioral and social sciences frequently leads to uninterpretable differences in the data obtained. For example, in behavioral and social science, it is difficult to specify as explicitly as in physical science just how an experiment should be replicated and how "exact" an experimental replication is sufficient. Thus it is often hard to establish whether "error" actually occurred or whether the specific conditions of the study differed sufficiently by chance to account for a difference in outcome. There is the additional problem that experimental replications are carried out on a different sample of research participants, which we know may differ markedly from the original sample. The steel balls rolled down inclined planes to demonstrate the laws of motion are much more dependably similar to one another than are human participants, who by their actions are to demonstrate the laws of learning.

The "cheater problem" in survey research (i.e., when a field interviewer fabricates the response to a question that was never asked of the respondent) is an example of intentional error in social science. A systematic attempt to assess the frequency and degree of interviewer cheating was reported by Hyman and his associates.[19] Fifteen interviewers were employed to conduct a study, and unbeknownst to them, each interviewed one or more planted respondents. One planted respondent, for example, was a "punctilious liberal"; he always qualified his responses so that no clear coding of his responses was possible. Another planted respondent played the role of a "hostile bigot"; he was uncooperative, suspicious, and unpleasant and tried to avoid committing himself to any answer at all on many of the questions. Interviews of the planted respondents were taped without the interviewers' knowledge. It was in the interview of the hostile bigot that the most cheating errors occurred. Four of the interviewers fabricated a great deal of the interview information they reported. These interviewers also cheated more on their interviews of the punctilious liberal, although in general there was less cheating in that interview. The frequency of cheating, then, bore some relation to the specific data-collection situation and was predictable from one situation to another.

In science generally, an assumption is made about the predictability of intentional error and is manifested in the distrust of data reported by an investigator who has been known, with varying degrees of certainty, to have erred intentionally on some other occasion. In science, a worker is allowed only once to contribute to the common data pool a bit of intentionally erring data. We should not, however, equate the survey research interviewer with the laboratory scientist or the scientist's assistants. The interviewer in survey research is frequently a part-time employee, less well trained, often less intelligent, and also less interested in the scientific implications of the data collected than are the scientist or the students and assistants who work with the scientist. Rarely does the survey research interviewer identify with a scientific career role or endorse its strong taboos against data fabrication or other intentional errors, and its strong insistence on accurate, uncontaminated data.[20]

A case of suspected fraud in psychology came to light in the 1970s, involving Sir Cyril Burt, the famous British psychologist whose work on twins had figured prominently in the debate about racial differences in intelligence.[21] A leader in the eugenics movement in England, Burt believed that intelligence was irredeemably determined by heredity, and he produced mountains of data to support this conviction. But it is thought that he fabricated his data, a suspicion that was first raised by Leon Kamin, who voiced skepticism about Burt's published findings after discovering internal implausibilities and basic methodological oversights in the data.[22] Extensive investigations undertaken by a British journalist reported a failure to find any evidence that Burt's two chief coauthors had ever existed, and he stands accused of having invented these phantom collaborators to lend credibility to his reports.[23] Because Burt is dead, we may never know whether the statistical artifacts in his reported data were due only to his carelessness or, as argued by Kamin and others, to a premeditated attempt to distort the research evidence.[24]

There are other famous examples of intentional error in the sciences. In the 19th century, Gregor Mendel, the legendary Austrian botanist, performed experiments that became the basis of the modern science of genetics. Working with garden peas, he showed how their characteristics could be predicted from the characteristics of their "parents." In a famous piece of scientific detective work, Ronald A. Fisher (the inventor of the F test and the null hypothesis) used the chi-square statistic to ask whether Mendel's data may have been manipulated so that they would seem to be more in line with his theory. Using the chi-square as a "goodness-of-fit" test of Mendel's reported findings compared with statistically expected values, Fisher found Mendel's "findings" *too perfect* to be plausible. Fisher concluded that Mendel had been deceived by a research assistant who knew what Mendel wanted to find and who manipulated the data *too* well.

Biosocial Attributes of Investigators

The physical and biological sciences have provided us with illustrations of investigator biases that do not influence the materials studied. We now turn to investigator artifacts that do influence the materials studied. A useful distinction is that between reactive measures and nonreactive measures; these terms are used to differentiate measurements that do (reactive) from those that do not (nonreactive) affect the behavior being measured. For example, in a study on therapy for weight control, the initial weigh-in may be a reactive stimulus to weight reduction, even without a therapeutic intervention.[25]

Robert E. Lana drew an analogy between the reactive nature of many psychological measures and Werner Heisenberg's principle of uncertainty.[26] This principle of quantum mechanics states that the precise measurement of one of two related, observable quantities will produce uncertainties in the measurement of the other quantity. Lana's thesis was that directly measuring behavior can introduce "uncertainties" into the measurements, a problem that increases as the measures become more precise. He mentioned a related situation in biology discussed by the physicist Neils Bohr.[27] To have precise knowledge of the living cell, we must examine its molecular structure, Bohr noted. However, such an examination destroys the life of the cell; thus life precludes the precise determination of its physiochemical nature.

It is perhaps harder to find examples in the physical and biological sciences of how differences among *investigators* may influence the materials studied. The speed of light, the reaction of one chemical with another, the arrangement of chromosomes within a cell—none of these are very likely to be affected by individual differences among the investigators interested in them. However, as we move from physics, chemistry, and molecular biology to those disciplines concerned with larger biological systems, we encounter more instances in which certain attributes of individual investigators can affect their research participants. By the time we reach the level of the behavioral and social sciences, there can be no doubt that investigators' differences may unintentionally affect the behavior in which they are interested. For example, one researcher reported that experienced observers in an animal laboratory could judge which of several experimenters had been handling a rat by the animal's behavior while running a maze or when being picked up.[28] Another researcher observed that a dog's heart rate would drop dramatically simply because a certain experimenter was present.[29]

Our focus in the remainder of this chapter is on the nature of individual differences among experimenters that have been shown to have unintentional effects on the responses of their participants. We begin with biosocial attributes (e.g., sex, age, ethnicity, and race).[30] For example, male and female experimenters may conduct the "same" experiment quite differently, so that the different results they obtain may be due to unintentionally different manipulations.[31] In an illustrative study, the interactions between experimenters and participants were recorded on sound films. It was found that only 12% of the experimenters ever smiled at their male participants, whereas 70% of the experimenters smiled at their female participants. Smiling by the experimenters, it was noted, affected the participants' responses. From this evidence and from some more detailed analyses, which suggest that female participants may be more protectively treated by their experimenters,[32] it appears that chivalry is not dead in the psychological experiment—a finding that may be heartening or disheartening to readers, but that is certainly interesting psychologically and disconcerting methodologically.

Another relevant finding is that male experimenters who work with female participants, and female experimenters who work with male participants, usually require more time to collect portions of their data than do male or female experimenters working with participants of their own sex.[33] Other interesting effects were revealed in the sound motion pictures of experimenters contacting participants. There was a tendency for male experimenters' movements to show greater friendliness than their tone of voice, and for male experimenters to be somewhat unfriendly toward male participants in the auditory channel of communication. The female experimenters were quite friendly toward their female participants in the visual channel but not in the auditory channel. Such research implies that the sex of the experimenter and the sex of the participant jointly determine how the experimenter conducts the research.[34]

Psychosocial Attributes of Investigators

Experimenters who differ along such measurable personal and social dimensions as anxiety, need for approval, status, and warmth also tend to obtain different responses from their research participants.[35] But what do the more anxious experimenters do that leads their participants to respond differently? It was found in one study that experimenters scoring higher on the Taylor Manifest Anxiety Scale were more fidgety and had a less dominant tone of voice.[36] Just what effects such behavior of the experimenter will have on the participants' responses may depend on the particular experiment being conducted and on the characteristics of the participants. In any case, we must assume that a more anxious experimenter cannot conduct exactly the same experiment as a less anxious experimenter. When an experiment has been conducted by a single experimenter, the probability of its successful replication by a second experimenter may depend on the similarity in personality of the two experimenters.

Anxiety is only one of the psychosocial experimenter variables affecting the participants' responses in an unintended way. In pioneering research on social desirability bias, Douglas P. Crowne and David Marlowe found that participants who scored high on a scale of need for approval tended to behave in such a way as to gain the approval of the experimenter.[37] There is evidence that experimenters who score high on this measure also behave so as to gain approval from their participants. An analysis of filmed interactions showed that experimenters scoring higher on the Marlowe-Crowne scale spoke to their participants in a more enthusiastic and affable tone of voice. In addition, these experimenters smiled more often and slanted their bodies more toward the participants than did experimenters who scored lower in the need for social approval.[38]

Earlier research in a clinical setting had shown that the examiners' power to control their patients' fate was a partial determinant of the patients' Rorschach responses; the status of the examiners, independent of their power to control the patient's destiny, had little effect.[39] In a different setting, we might suppose that a Roman Catholic priest would obtain different responses to personal questions asked of Roman Catholic respondents than would a Roman Catholic layperson. That was the question addressed in another experiment, in which a layman and a priest, each garbed sometimes as a layman and sometimes as a priest, asked a series of personal questions of male and female participants.[40] The results were complex but interesting, male and female participants responding differently not so much to priest versus layman as to whether the priest and the layman were playing their true roles or simulating those roles.[41]

Experimenters with a warmer manner and "cooler" experimenters have also been found to obtain different responses from participants.[42] Working with children, researchers found that their participants' judgments of affect in photographs were influenced by the degree of friendliness shown by the data collectors.[43] In one study, within-experimenter variation was a powerful unintended determinant of participants' responses.[44] In this study, the variations in feeling state of a particular data collector were found to be related to his participants' physiological reactions. When the experimenter had a "bad day," his participants' heart rates showed greater acceleration than when he had a "good day." Surprisingly, no relation was found between the data collector's feeling state and his own physiological responses.

Situational Factors

More than an experimenter's score on a test of anxiety, his or her status and warmth are defined and determined by the nature of the experimental situation and the participants being contacted. For example, the degree of warmth an experimenter shows one participant may be correlated with the degree of warmth that the experimenter shows other participants. Whether the experimenter inadvertently encounters a participant with whom he or she has had prior social contact is another situational variable. In fact, the degree of acquaintanceship between experimenter and participant, the experimenter's level of experience, and the things that happen to the experimenter before and during his or her interaction with the participant have all been shown to affect the participant's responses.[45]

One study found that experimenters who were acquainted with and open to their participants obtained not only the more open responses we might expect on the basis of reciprocity, but also superior performance in a paired-associate learning task.[46] In an earlier study, by Eleanor L. Sacks, 30 children, all about 3 years old, were divided into three experimental groups. Sacks spent one hour each day for 10 days with the children of one group in a nursery school, participating as a good, interested teacher. With the children of the second group, she spent the same amount of time, but her role was that of a dull, uninterested teacher. She had no prior contact with the third group of children. The results were defined as changes in intelligence test scores before and after treatment. The IQ gains were 14.5 points in the first group, 5.0 points in the second group, and 1.6 points in the third group. This study illustrates not only the effects of prior contact, but also the effects of the warmth of that contact. When the experimenter had played a "warmer" role, the gain in IQ was 9.5 IQ points greater than when she had played a "cooler" role.[47]

Previously, we mentioned that the kind of person the experimenter is *before* entering the experiment may affect the responses of the participants. There is also evidence that the kind of person the experimenter becomes *after* entering the experiment may alter his or her behavior and, in turn, may affect the responses of the participants. In the folklore of psychologists who conduct experiments, there is the notion that sometimes, perhaps more often than we would expect, prospective participants contacted early in an experiment behave differently in the research from participants recruited later. There may be something to this bit of lore, even if we make sure that people seen earlier and later in an experiment come from the same population. The difference may lie in changes over the course of the study in the behavior of the experimenter. From what we know of performance curves, we might predict both a practice effect and a fatigue effect on the experimenter.

For example, in experiments in which the participants were asked to rate stimulus persons, the experimenter-participant interactions were filmed and then analyzed by judges. It was found that the experimenters became more accurate and faster in their reading of instructions to their later-contacted participants. In addition, the experimenters became more bored or less interested over the course of the experiment, as coded from their behavior in the experimental interaction. As we might also predict, the experimenters became less tense with more experience. These changes in the experimenters' behavior during the course of the experiment appeared to affect their participants' responses. Those participants contacted by experimenters whose behavior had changed in the ways described rated the experimenters as less successful.[48]

The experimenter-participant communication system is a complex of intertwining feedback loops. The experimenter's behavior, we have seen, affects the participant's responses. The participant's responses also affect the experimenter's behavior, which in turn affects the participant's responses. In this way, the participants play an indirect part in the determination of their own responses.[49] In one study, half the student experimenters had their hypotheses confirmed by their first few participants, who were actually accomplices of the principal investigator. The remaining student experimenters had their hypotheses disconfirmed. This confirmation or disconfirmation of their hypotheses affected the experimenters' behavior enough so that, from their next participants, who were bona fide and not accomplices, they obtained different responses not only to the experimental task, but on standard tests of personality as well. These responses were predictable from a knowledge of the responses that the student experimenters had obtained from the accomplices (i.e., the earlier-contacted participants).[50]

An interesting footnote on the psychology of the accomplice comes from this experiment. The accomplices had been coached in the responses they were to give the student experimenter. However, they did not know when they were confirming or disconfirming an experimenter's hypothesis or, indeed, that there were expectancies to be confirmed at all. Despite their coaching, the accomplices' performance was affected by the student experimenters' expectancies, that is, by whether the student experimenter's hypothesis was being confirmed or disconfirmed by their responses. Thus we can also think of the accomplices as "experimenters" and the student experimenters as the accomplices' targets or "victims." As targets of the accomplices, the student experimenters were no more passive responders than were the accomplices: they "acted back"—so it is good to think of them also as participants.

There are, of course, many other ways in which situational factors may intervene. For example, the physical scene in which the experiment takes place may affect the participant's responses, as Henry W. Riecken pointed out.[51] Riecken noted how little was known about how the scene affects the participant's responses and how the laboratory setting affects the experimenter. Riecken wondered about the effect on his participants of the experimenter's white coat. Perhaps it made the experimenter seem more of a scientist in the participants' eyes, and perhaps it also made the experimenter feel more like a scientist. If "clothes make the man," a respectable-looking laboratory should make the scientist (male *or* female) feel more the part. The most senior of the laboratory directors may not be susceptible to such an effect, but most senior investigators do not actually collect data themselves. It is far more common for data to be collected by subordinates, who may be more influenced by the kind of setting in which they contact the participants.

We do not want to leave readers with a princess-and-the-pea image of research participants as overly sensitive and overly responsive to the slightest situational variations. It is possible for even the most outrageous circumstances to have no biasing effect, and it is not easy to foresee when biasing effects will actually materialize.[52] In a classic case, H. B. Hovey had an intelligence test administered to 171 people divided into two groups.[53] One group took the test in a quiet room, and the other took it in a room with seven bells, five buzzers, a 550-watt spotlight, a 90,000-volt rotary-spark gap, a phonograph, two organ pipes of varying pitch, three metal whistles, a 55-pound circular saw mounted on a wooden frame, a photographer taking pictures, and four students doing acrobatics! The events in the second room were choreographed so that a number of these distractions sometimes occurred concurrently and at other times the room was quiet. The surprising result was that the group in the second room scored as well as the group in the first.

Modeling Effects

The term *modeling* means that someone who observes someone else (a model) demonstrate a certain behavior then copies the behavior. For example, in behavior therapy based on modeling, the clients observe someone demonstrating the ideal behavior and receiving rewards for it. The client makes the association that copying the ideal behavior will result in rewards for him or her, and in this way, observational learning occurs. An application would be the use of this treatment for agoraphobia, which is a fear of open spaces, crowds, streets, and traveling. The agoraphobic might observe a close friend who manages to stay calm under conditions that would normally cause the agoraphobic to panic. Modeling, as we see next, is also a potential source of interactional artifacts in behavioral research.

In survey research, there is considerable evidence that the interviewer's own opinion, attitude, or ideology affects the responses of those interviewed. The respondent may try to copy what he or she thinks the interviewer believes, although the basic paradigm used to study this modeling phenomenon is not without its own potential artifacts. The basic paradigm has been to ask the interviewers who are to be used in a given project to respond to the questionnaire themselves. How they have responded is then correlated with the responses that they obtain from those interviewed. The problem is that, if the interviewers are allowed any choice in the selection of the interviewees, they may select like-minded respondents.

Even if the interviewers are not allowed any choice in interviewee selection, but the respondents are not randomly assigned to interviewers, the same problem may result. For example, if the interviewers are assigned a sample of respondents from their home neighborhoods, the opinions of interviewers and respondents are likely to come "precorrelated" because opinions are related to neighborhoods. However, if the respondents are randomly assigned to the interviewers, and if errors of observation, recording, and coding can be eliminated (at least statistically), the resulting correlation between the interviewers' opinions and their respondents' opinions provides a good measure of modeling effects. Such studies suggest that interviewer modeling effects cannot be expected always to occur or to produce substantial bias.[54] In a minority of studies, there has even been evidence of negative modeling; that is, the participants have responded in a direction opposite to that seemingly favored by the interviewer.[55]

An early study, reported by Hyman and his associates, illustrates this area of research; the data were collected by the Audience Research Institute in 1940.[56] The research participants were given a very brief description of a proposed motion-picture plot and were asked to state whether they would like to see such a movie. Both male and female interviewers contacted both male and female participants. The results were that the responses obtained by the interviewers depended on their gender and, seemingly, on the respondents' inference of what movies the interviewers would, because of their gender, probably enjoy most. One of the film plots described was that of *Lawrence of Arabia*. When male and female participants were asked about this film by interviewers of their own gender, the male participants were 50% more likely than female participants to favor the film. When the interviewer was of the opposite gender, the male participants responded favorably only 14% more often than female participants. It appeared that the participants responded by "preferring" those movies which, judging by the gender of the interviewer, they thought they *should* prefer.

An interesting question is whether participants in field research or laboratory research tend, in general, to respond so as to reduce the perceived differences between themselves and the data collector with whom they are interacting. No decisive answer to this question is yet available, and surely, as an assertion, it is highly oversimplified. It may, however, be a reasonable one if both the participants' attributes and the nature of the data collection situation are considered. From all we know at present, these factors are likely to combine with the participants' motives to be less different from the data collector. Two sources of such motives are obvious. One is the wish to be similar in order to smooth the social interaction. The other is the wish to be more like a person who seems to enjoy, either continuously or at least situationally, a position of higher status. To "keep up with" that Jones who is a data collector, one must behave as one believes a Jones would behave in that situation.

We mentioned how modeling is used in behavioral therapy to reshape people's behavior. Modeling effects may also occur unintentionally in clinical practice. It is often said of clinical psychological interactions that the clinicians model their patients somewhat after the image the clinicians have of themselves. When the clinical interaction is the protracted one of psychotherapy, it seems especially easy to believe that such effects may occur. If it is plausible that participants in research tend to respond as they believe the experimenter would respond, then it is also plausible that such effects occur when the "participant" is a client or patient, who may have all the modeling motives of the experimental participant and, in addition, the powerful motive of hope that his or her distress will be relieved.

Clinical psychologist Stanley R. Graham reported a study in which 10 psychotherapists were divided into two groups on the basis of their own perceptual style of approach to the Rorschach blots.[57] Half the therapists tended to perceive more movement in the inkblots relative to color than did the remaining therapists, who tended to perceive more color. The therapists saw a total of 89 patients for eight months of treatment. Rorschachs administered to the patients of the two groups of therapists showed no differences before treatment. After treatment, the patients seen by the more movement-perceiving therapists perceived more movement themselves. Patients seen by the more color-perceiving therapists perceived more color after treatment. Such evidence suggests the possible occurrence of unintentional modeling in the psychotherapeutic relationship.[58]

Studies have suggested that modeling effects occur even in structured experimental interactions. A study in educational psychology found that high-authoritarian experimenters were unable to convince their participants of the value of nonauthoritarian teaching methods.[59] Presumably, such experimenters could not convincingly persuade participants to accept communications that the experimenters themselves found unacceptable. Another researcher used a phrase association task and found that participants contacted by experimenters showing a higher degree of associative disturbance also showed a higher degree of disturbance than did participants contacted by experimenters showing less disturbance.[60] Even before such experiments had been conducted, Floyd H. Allport had expressed the idea that experimenters may suggest to participants, quite unintentionally, the experimenters' own appraisal of the experimental stimulus, and that this suggestion may affect the results of the experiment.[61]

In a series of 10 experiments, the occurrence and magnitude of modeling effects were assessed in a laboratory setting.[62] The studies, conducted between 1959 and 1964, used a person perception task in which 900 participants were asked by student experimenters to rate a series of photos on how successful or unsuccessful the persons pictured appeared to be. As part of their training, the 161 student experimenters rated the photos before contacting their participants. In each study, the modeling effects were defined by the correlation between the mean rating of the photos by the different student experimenters and the mean photo rating obtained by each experimenter from all his or her participants. An analysis, in which the correlations were combined without being weighted in any way, produced a mean correlation of +.15; another analysis, in which the correlations were combined after each was weighted by the number of student experimenters per study, produced a mean correlation of +.14. These overall results were in the direction predicted by a modeling hypothesis.[63] Thus, from all the evidence that is available, it seems that modeling effects occur at least sometimes in psychological research conducted in the field or laboratory.[64]

Coping with Investigator Biases

We have described the existence of several different types of experimenter biases, and in the next chapter, we will focus on one additional class of interactional artifacts, those attributable to the investigator's expectancies. We will have more to say about how such effects can be controlled, but generally speaking, the most critical control is woven into the fabric of science by the tradition of replication. For example, frequent replication of observations serves to establish the definition of observer bias. It does not, however, eliminate that problem; it was long ago recognized by Karl Pearson that replicated observations made under similar conditions of anticipation, instrumentation, and psychological climate may, by virtue of their intercorrelation, all be biased with respect to some external criterion.[65] An excellent example was the infamous case of the N rays. Until they were finally debunked by R. W. Wood, they had been "observed" by many scientists, and only a few scientists had been unable to detect the phenomenon.

The human mind, as Lavoisier was quoted earlier as saying, does indeed get "creased into a way of seeing things."[66] Karl Popper's principle of falsifiability (refutability) is also relevant here.[67] As he noted, it is quite possible for anyone with a fertile imagination to "observe" things that are consistent with almost any claims. Good hypotheses in science must be risky, Popper advised. To be scientific, claims have to be refutable by some conceivable observation, not merely confirmable by those who, as F. W. Lane was previously quoted as saying, "equate what they *think* they see, and sometimes what they *want* to see, with what actually happens."[68]

In the case of interpreter bias, some of these confounding effects are fully public events and some are not. If we have public observations that are not congenial with our own views, we are always free to disagree. It is the public nature of the interpretive differences which ensures that, in time, they will be adequately addressed and will perhaps be resolved with the addition of new observations or the development of new mental matrices that allow the reconciliation of opposing views. But when interpreter biases operate to keep observations off the market, they are less than fully public events. For example, if an observation is discarded because the investigator believes it was made in error, no one can disagree and attempt to use the discordancy in a reformulation of an existing theory or as evidence against its tenability. When statistically nonsignificant results are unpublishable, the fact of their statistical nonsignificance is not a publicly available observation. When sensitive or unpopular results cannot be published, they are kept out of the public data pool of science. Thus, to the extent that the "public-ness" of science is encouraged, we can control to some extent for interpreter bias.

We also discussed specific allegations of fraud (intentional error). The whistle blower's charge of fraud is such a serious one that it is leveled only at the peril of the accuser, and it is essential that the facts be known. The charge may be quite legitimate, in which case it must be fully aired, and steps must be taken to correct the situation. However, it is possible for anonymous accusers to create mischief with false allegations. The accuser might, for example, be a vengeful former student or employee who wants to hoodwink a nervous administrator into acting wrongly and precipitously against an innocent individual. Even an unfounded allegation can take on a life of its own. Thus it is essential to gather the relevant facts because, once started, a false allegation is hard to stop.

Making one's data available to others would be a very useful convention, although it is necessary to protect the identity and privacy of the respondents so that we do not violate any ethical dictates or inadvertently cause respondents embarrassment.[69] If there is ever to be an open-books system, the borrower must make it convenient for the lender. A request to "send me all your data on verbal conditioning" to a scientist who has been collecting data on that subject for 10 years rightly winds up being ignored. If data are reasonably requested, if the reason for the request is given as an accompanying courtesy, and if the identity of the people who participated is protected, the data can be duplicated at the borrower's expense and given to the borrower on the stipulation that there will be no ethical violations. Such a data-sharing system would serve to allay any doubts about the extent and type of errors in a set of data. It would provide the borrower something very useful that may not have been of interest to the original data collector.

In general, the most basic control for experimenter biases is, again, the tradition of replication of research findings. J. B. Conant drew a compelling analogy between the scientist and the person trying to unlock a door with a set of previously untried keys. The person says, "If this key fits the lock, the lock will spring when I turn the key."[70] The scientist has a choice of "keys" (research methods), decides on one, and says in essence, "Let's try it." Conant's point was that the scientific outlook relies on methods that independent investigators can use to replicate what others have opened up for scrutiny and investigation. It is this reliance on independent replication that connects scientists in different fields, though they use different empirical methods in their research. In the behavioral sciences, the situation is perhaps more complicated. As mentioned previously, in work with human participants, there are sampling and procedural differences so trivial on the surface that few people would expect them to make a difference. However, it is to these differences that we turn in part to account for the different results of similar experiments. We require replications but often can conclude little from the failure to achieve confirming data.[71] Science, it is said, is self-correcting, but in the behavioral sciences, it corrects itself only very slowly.

Chapter 3

Expectations as Self-Fulfilling Prophecies

I am human, said the poet, nothing human is foreign to me; self-awareness requires no less an admission and self-esteem no less an aspiration on the part of the behavioral scientist. But the more involved he is with his subject-matter, the more likely it is that his observations will be affected by the involvement.

—Abraham Kaplan[1]

Expectancy Bias

We have seen cases from science and everyday life in which suppositions and expectations influenced what people believed they saw, so that in some cases they "observed" something that was not actually there (e.g., N rays). People may also reach false conclusions based on false assumptions because they see something and misinterpret it. In 1954, residents of Seattle, Washington, panicked at what they perceived to be "pittings" on their automobile windshields, supposedly caused by radioactive fallout from the Eniwetok H-bomb tests.[2] The "pits" turned out to be harmless little black particles that had formed through the improper combustion of bituminous coal. Sometimes people *act* on assumptions that ultimately turn out to be false. The way stock prices spike or drop precipitously on the basis of a false rumor is a case in point.[3] Frequently people's wishes for, or expectations of, an event lead them to behave in a way that increases the likelihood the event will occur as expected; the name of this phenomenon is *self-fulfilling prophecy*.

The term was coined by sociologist Robert K. Merton,[4] who explained the self-fulfilling prophecy by means of a parable about a bank (the "Last National Bank") that was a flourishing institution until its depositers cleared out their accounts after hearing a rumor that the bank was insolvent: "Once the depositers questioned the validity of the economic structure on which the bank was built, the structure lost its validity and ruin was the result."[5] Gordon W. Allport argued that self-fulfilling prophecies explain why nations that expect to go to war often have their expectations confirmed,[6] and Kenneth B. Clark said they explain the predicament of impoverished African-American children, whom he characterized as victims of an "educational self-fulfilling prophecy."[7] In George Bernard Shaw's play *Pygmalion*—which was made into the Broadway musical *My Fair Lady*—Eliza Doolittle becomes the object of a self-fulfilling prophecy. A poor street girl who sells flowers, she captures the attention of Henry Higgins, a language professor, because she has the most atrocious accent he has ever heard. He bets that, by changing her accent, he can transform her into a "lady" in English high society. He wins his bet and imagines himself as the ancient Greek sculptor, Pygmalion, who created a statue of a woman so lovely he could not resist her.

Some prophecy of how the investigation will turn out is also virtually a constant in science. Behavioral researchers, like other scientists generally, conduct research specifically to test hypotheses or expectations about the nature of things. When the researcher's hypothesis or expectation leads unintentionally to behavior toward the research participants that increases the likelihood that the researcher's expectation will be confirmed, we call this an *expectancy effect.* In this chapter we will discuss studies of expectancy effects as well as methods of controlling the bias that results from these effects (expectancy bias). Expectancy effects have also been experimentally manipulated in the classroom, and we will review how expectancies of teachers may produce so-called Pygmalion effects in their pupils' intellectual performance.

A Sample of Studies

The systematic study of expectancy bias in research started in the late 1950s. The idea for these studies had a lot to do with serendipity, which means a lucky discovery—it comes from Serendip, once the name for Sri Lanka, because it was said that the three princes of Serendip made lucky discoveries. The idea for a series of studies of expectancy effects was inspired by a serendipitous result in Rosenthal's dissertation research. It led to a frantic search of the literature for an explanation and to the term *unconscious experimenter bias,* which evolved into the concept of *experimenter expectancy bias* and also a series of studies at the University of North Dakota (UND), with Kermit L. Fode, of how experimenters' hypotheses can unwittingly influence their results.[8]

In the initial studies at UND, student experimenters instructed their participants to judge and rate the success or failure of people by looking at their photos. Half the experimenters were led to expect success ratings by their participants, while the remaining experimenters were led to expect failure ratings from their participants.[9] The results of the studies were consistent with this expectancy induction: ratings of success predominated in the success condition, and ratings of failure prevailed in the failure condition. When these results were submitted to a journal for publication, they were met with ambivalence; accordingly, further studies using animal and human subjects were undertaken.

In the first study of expectancy effects in animal learning, a dozen student experimenters at UND taught rats to run a maze with the aid of visual cues.[10] The rats were randomly assigned to the students. Half the students were told their rats had been bred for "maze-brightness," and the other half were told their rats had been bred for "maze-dullness." There were no differences in the rats except the experimenters' expectations. At the end of the study, the results were clear. The rats run by experimenters expecting brighter behavior showed significantly better learning than the rats run by experimenters expecting dull behavior.

This experiment was repeated at Ohio State University, with Reed Lawson the coinvestigator, this time using a series of learning trials in a Skinner box.[11] Half of the student experimenters were told their rats were "Skinner-box-bright," and the other half were told their rats were "Skinner-box-dull." Once again, there were not really any differences in the two groups of rats, at least not until the results were analyzed at the end of the study: then, the allegedly brighter animals really were "brighter" and the alleged dullards were more "dull."

Neither of the animal studies showed any evidence that the student experimenters might have falsified their results. Thus it could be concluded that the experimenters' expectations had acted not on the experimenters' evaluation of the animals' performance, but on the actual performance of the rats. If rats behaved more "brightly" when so expected by their experimenters, it seemed plausible that children might behave more brightly if so expected by their teacher. Educational theorists had, after all, been saying for a long time that some children were unable to learn because their teachers expected them to be unable to learn. Was it possible that a teacher who believed that certain pupils were especially bright might act more warmly toward them, teach them more material, and spend more time with them? Would the teacher's belief thereby become a self-fulfilling prophecy?

A felicitous opportunity to address these questions arose when a letter arrived from Lenore Jacobson, the principal of a South San Francisco elementary school.[12] Jacobson told of her interest in the problem of teacher expectations and ended her letter, "If you ever 'graduate' to classroom children, please let me know whether I can be of assistance." It was an offer too good to pass up, and in the spring of 1964, all the children in Jacobson's school were administered a nonverbal test of intelligence, disguised as a test that would predict "intellectual blooming."[13] There were 18 classrooms in the school; each of the six grade levels had 3, composed of children with above-average, average, or below-average ability. In each of the 18 classrooms, approximately 20% of the children were chosen at random to form the experimental group, and each teacher was given the names of these children in his or her class. The teacher was told that these children's scores on the "test of intellectual blooming" indicated that they would show remarkable gains in intellectual competence during the next eight months of school. The only actual difference between the experimental-group and the control-group children was in the mind of their teacher.

Eight months later, all the children were retested with the same IQ test, and those children from whom the teachers had been led to expect greater intellectual gains showed, over all, a greater gain in IQ scores than did the children in the control group. Although the greatest differential gain in total IQ appeared after one school year, the experimental group clearly held an advantage over the other children, the controls, even after two years.

These studies give a flavor of the research on expectancy effects, though they barely scratch the surface of this area. Other studies include Peter Blanck's work on the effects of expectancies held by judges and juries,[14] Marylee Taylor's work on how interpersonal expectancies can perpetuate racial injustice,[15] Dov Eden's investigations of interpersonal expectations in the workplace,[16] Howard Friedman's and Robin DiMatteo's work on expectations in health maintenance,[17] and Elisha Babad's studies of the "golem effect."[18] The Golem is a kind of Frankenstein's monster in Jewish mythology; Babad's research examines the often self-fulfilling nature of teachers' negative expectancies about some of their students.

The First 345 Studies

For a number of years, the central question in the study of expectancy effects was whether they even existed. This question stimulated a spate of studies in a range of settings, such as investigations of symbol learning, athletic performance, the ability to discriminate tones, changes in IQ scores, and learning in mazes and Skinner boxes. In the decade after the first expectancy study, over 100 studies of interpersonal expectations had been reported. By the following decade, the number had risen to 345 experiments, and by the beginning of the 1990s, there were over 450 studies. We next sample some of the data from a meta-analysis of the 345 studies done through the 1970s, to sketch the overall expectancy effect and the specific effects of expectancies in eight domains of behavioral research.

The term *meta-analysis* means an "analysis of analyses," or a collective reanalysis of previously reported results. Employing this approach, Rosenthal and Donald B. Rubin first examined the proportion of studies showing expectancy biases in eight research domains.[19] This analysis was designed to determine how many of the predicted results were significant at "*p* equal to or less than .05." The assumption was that, if the 345 had been a randomly selected sample of studies from a population of all possible studies for which the null hypothesis was true, we should expect 5% of the studies to achieve .05 significance by chance alone. The first column of numbers in Table 3.1 shows that all the proportions exceeded the expected value, and that the median proportion of .39 is almost eight times larger than the expected chance value.

Still, some unknown factors might have kept any negative results out of sight so that only these 345 studies were accessible. For example, studies that failed to find statistically significant results might have been filed away in obscurity, a possibility called the *file-drawer problem*. The implication is that the 345 might have been a biased sample of studies. One way to address

Table 3.1

Expectancy Effects in Eight Areas

Research area	Proportion of results that reached $p < .05$ in the predicted direction	Mean effect size in Cohen's d	Mean effect size in Pearson r
Laboratory interviews	.38	0.14	.07
Reaction time	.22	0.17	.08
Learning and ability	.29	0.54	.26
Person perception	.27	0.55	.27
Inkblot tests	.44	0.84	.39
Everyday situations	.40	0.88	.40
Psychophysical judgments	.43	1.05	.46
Animal learning	.73	1.73	.65
Median	.39	0.70	.33

this concern was to compute the overall p of the 345 studies and ask how many additional studies with null results it would take to boost this p value to a "barely acceptable" level of significance.[20] Finding that it would take only a small number of studies would imply that the overall p could be easily upset by a few null results tucked away in file drawers. Finding that it would take a large number of studies to overturn the obtained p value would assure us that the file-drawer problem was not a concern in this case. Many researchers and editors regard "$p = .05$" as a cutoff, or barely acceptable, level of significance.[21] In this case, it was found that it would take more than 65,000 studies with null results to move the overall p associated with an expectancy effect in the 345 studies to a barely acceptable $p = .05$.

Other analyses of the 345 studies concentrated on the size of the expectancy relationship (called the effect size) rather than only on probability values. Even small effects may have associated p values that are statistically significant, and even large effects may have associated p values that are not statistically significant. The reason is that t tests, F tests, chi-square tests, Z tests, and so on can be shown to consist of two components—one reflecting the effect size and the other, the sample size. These two components are related in a way that can be described by a simple conceptual equation: Magnitude of significance test = Size of effect × Size of study (where "Size of study" can be defined as the sample size).

This conceptual relationship teaches us that a significance test will have a larger value—and therefore will be associated with a smaller (i.e., "more significant") p value—with increases in the effect size or the sample size. Researchers can consult a table to determine how large a sample they will need to detect a given effect at a preferred significance level.[22] Because the effect size and the significance level tell us different things, it is prudent to consider both pieces of information. Table 3.2 shows four possible outcomes of p values and effect sizes, and it implies how easily we can fall into the trap of making spurious conclusions when we do not understand what p values really tell us. The "acceptable" and "unacceptable" labels imply that the particular values of an effect size or a significance level considered "large enough" or sufficiently stringent to detect the presence of a "real" effect or a "real" difference are not cut in stone.

Suppose we found a "nonsignificant" p and a "large" effect size—what would this tell us? If we merely concluded on the basis of the significance level that "nothing happened," we might be making a serious mistake. A small sample size may have led to failure to detect the obtained effect at the preferred p level; this research should be continued with a larger sample size before we

Table 3.2

Potential Problems of Inference as a Function of Obtained
Effect Sizes and Significance Levels

	Effect size	
	---	---
Level of significance	*"Acceptable"* *(large enough)*	*"Unacceptable"* *(too small)*
"Acceptable" (low enough)	No inferential problem	Mistaking statistical significance for practical importance
"Unacceptable" (too high)	Failure to perceive practical importance of "nonsignificant" results	No inferential problem

embrace the null hypothesis as "true." Suppose we found a "significant" *p* and a "small" effect—what would this tell us? The answer depends both on the sample size and on what we consider the practical importance of the estimated effect size. With a large sample size, we may mistake a result that is merely "very significant" for one that is of practical importance.

One informative measure of the effect size when there are two groups to be compared is Jacob Cohen's *d* statistic. It is computed by dividing the difference between the group means by the population standard deviation; the result tells us the difference between the means in standard normal curve units. If $d = 0$, there is no difference; if $d = 1.0$, the difference is equivalent to one standard deviation in a normal curve (which would be a very substantial difference).

Another informative measure of effect size is the Pearson r. In the case of two groups, we code the groups (e.g., 0 and 1) and then correlate each participant's group membership with the person's score on the dependent variable; the result tells us the magnitude of the relationship between the independent and dependent variables in correlational units. If $r = 0$, there is no such relationship; if $r = 1.0$, group membership is a perfect predictor of scores on the dependent variable.

Even very small effects are sometimes important, so it is a good idea to examine the magnitude of the effect within the particular context of the variables in question. However, as a general rule of thumb, Cohen recommended that we call $d = 0.2$ or $r = .1$ a "small" effect; $d = 0.5$ or $r = .3$, a "medium" effect; and $d = 0.8$ or $r = .5$, a "large" effect. Table 3.1 shows d's and r's based on a stratified sample of the 345 studies.[23] Using Cohen's rules, we would say that the effect sizes ranged from "small" in laboratory interviews and reaction time studies to "very large" in psychophysical judgment and animal learning studies. The median d and r are comparable to effect sizes generally considered informative and reliable in behavioral science.

There were other analyses of the 345 studies, with further results consistent with the claim that expectancy bias is a real phenomenon. For example, another analysis was made of studies reported in doctoral dissertations and of studies reported in articles and other archives. The idea was that dissertations were more readily retrievable, less likely to be suppressed because of nonsignificant results, and more likely to meet at least minimum standards of quality. The median d for dissertations was 0.38 ("small to medium"), and for all other studies it was 0.82. Other analyses isolated studies in which there had been specific controls for cheating or recording errors; the median d in these studies was 0.48 ("medium"). Thus all the findings implied that expectancy effects had been frequently demonstrated in a wide range of settings.

Moderation of Interpersonal Expectancies

Over time, a picture has emerged about moderating variables that may influence the size of interpersonal expectancy effects. For example, in the case of teacher expectancy effects,[24] Stephen W. Raudenbush and A. S. Bryk analyzed 18 randomized replications of the Pygmalion experiment.[25] The replications generally involved an experimenter's giving a test to a randomly selected sample of students who were then identified to their teachers as likely to experience substantial intellectual growth. Raudenbush and Bryk found the size of the Pygmalion effect to be moderated by the amount of prior contact between the teachers and the students. The Pygmalion effect was not as likely to occur if the teacher had had prior contact with the student, perhaps because teacher's initial impressions may have hardened by the time they received the expectancy suggestion.

John M. Darley and Kathryn C. Oleson drew on a number of previous findings in order to theorize some conditions that may place limits on the expectancy effect.[26] For example, as in the role played by prior contact, the work of Edward E. Jones suggests that some trait impressions may be highly resistant to modification.[27] There is a saying that "first impressions count," but some first impressions count more than others.[28] Suppose, based on prior contact with some person, we think he is stupid or dishonest; such an impression may not be easily overcome.[29] Stereotypes rooted in prejudice may become so deeply ingrained that they are not easily excised merely by a prediction of change.[30]

Another condition, suggested in part by other work,[31] is the ability to understand expectancy cues. For example, more recent studies by Rosnow, Anne Skleder, Marianne Jaeger, and Bruce Rind have investigated the extent to which people are able to understand other's actions and intentions. We are not all equally endowed with such interpersonal acumen, and some actions and intentions seem intrinsically less transparent. The results of this research suggest a kind of built-in cognitive hierarchical structure, which is associated with the ability to read and interpret interpersonal cues.[32] If we generalize to expectancy cues, it follows that if a person is insensitive to certain expectancy cues, then they cannot be processed or the expectancies cannot take hold.

A third condition was implied in research by William B. Swann, in which he found that personality sometimes triumphs over expectancy.[33] A person who feels that he possesses a certain central trait is more likely to be perceived as really having that trait, regardless of any initial expectancy by others. The structure of the person's self-image hardens over time, as others accept the self-defined image as real and reinforce it (perhaps unwittingly) through their relations with the person. This is a different kind of self-fulfilling prophecy, a "competing prophecy," which is at odds with the expectancy cues and yet overcomes them in a uniquely self-fulfilling way.

Mediation of Interpersonal Expectancies

There has also been theoretical speculation on the mediating cues and behaviors by which interpersonal expectancy effects are communicated.[34] Many of the experiments on the operation of experimenter expectancy effects have used a standard photo-rating task, in which the participants were asked by their experimenter to rate the degree of success or failure that appeared to be reflected in photographed faces. One of the earliest and strongest hints that nonverbal cues are probably involved in the mediation of such expectancy effects came from the fact that all the experimenters had read the same standard instructions to their participants. Despite this standardization of the *verbal* content of the experimenters' communications, the participants' responses accorded with the expectations that had been experimentally induced in the minds of the experimenters. If the words in the instructions did not differ, then *nonverbal* cues must have been the critical elements. When a screen was placed between the experimenter and the research participant, the size of the effect of experimenter expectations was cut in half.

A two-stage study, conducted by John G. Adair and J. S. Epstein, lends support to the idea that interpersonal expectations may be communicated by the sender's tone of voice.[35] In Stage 1, the experimenters were led to expect either high or low ratings of success from the research participants. Just as in many other studies of this kind, the experimenters did in fact obtain results in the direction of their expectations. In Stage 2, there were no experimenters at all. Instead, the tape-recorded voices of the experimenters instructing the participants in Stage 1 were played for new groups of participants. Thus the Stage 2 participants were given their instructions not by "real" experimenters but by the voices of experimenters who had been given different expectations of how their participants should rate the presented photos. The results of Stage 2 showed that the effects of experimenters' expectations were just as effectively communicated by their tape-recorded voices as they had been when the experimenters had interacted directly with their participants in Stage 1. Audio cues, then, were again sufficient to communicate to the participants the expectations of their experimenters.

E. J. Zoble and R. S. Lehman found substantial effects of experimenter expectations in a tone-length discrimination task even when the participants were restricted to auditory cues.[36] This study went on to show, however, that visual cues alone could also mediate substantial effects of experimenter expectations in this task. Taken together, the results imply that, when participants are deprived of either visual or auditory information, they focus on the channel that is available to them. This greater attention, and perhaps greater effort, may enable people to extract more information from the single channel than they could, or would, from that same channel if the two channels were combined.

Teacher Expectancy Effects

Various studies underscore the importance of nonverbal cues in the mediation of teacher expectancy effects,[37] and interest has now concentrated on a four-factor model of the communication of expectancy cues. This model implies that teachers (perhaps also clinicians, supervisors, and employers) who expect superior performance from some of their pupils (clients, trainees, or employees) treat these "special" persons and the remaining "less special" persons differently in the following ways: First, teachers create a warmer socioemotional *climate* for their special students. This warmth is at least partially communicated by nonverbal cues. Second, teachers give their special students differentiated *feedback,* both verbal and nonverbal, about how these students have been performing. Third, teachers provide more *input* for the special students. That is, they teach more material, and more difficult material, to the special students. Fourth, there are more opportunities for *output,* or responding, by the special students. These opportunities are offered both verbally and nonverbally, for example, by giving the special student more time to answer a question.

A recent simplification of this four-factor model of teacher expectancy effects is called *affect-effort theory.*[38] This theory asserts that a change in the level of a teacher's expectations of the intellectual performance of a student is translated into (1) a change in the affect shown by the teacher toward that student and, relatively independently, (2) a change in the degree of effort exerted by the teacher in teaching that student. The more favorable the change in the teacher's level of expectation for a particular student, the more positive the affect shown toward that student and the greater the effort expended on the student's behalf. The increase in positive affect is theorized to reflect the teacher's increased liking of the student for any of several plausible reasons.[39] The increase in teaching effort is theorized to reflect the teacher's increased belief that the student is capable of learning, so that the effort is worth it.[40]

One aspect of this theory that is under study by Nalini Ambady has some fascinating implications. Ambady found that it was possible to predict the ratings of a college instructor's effectiveness over the course of an entire semester from an examination of a 30-second slice of teaching behavior. In this "thin slice" of behavior, the raters had access only to the silent videotape or the tone of voice (not the content) in which the instructor was communicating with students. These predictive correlations, often in the range of .6 to .7, have been replicated in high schools and fit very well with the results of many other studies of thin slices of nonverbal behavior.[41] Research is under way to examine other implications of affect-effort theory.[42]

Controls for Expectancy Effects

Table 3.3 lists a number of strategies for controlling the effects of experimenters' expectancies. First, with the sample size of participants fixed, the larger the sample of the experimenters, the smaller the subsample of participants that each data collector must contact. Subdivision of the experiment among several experimenters may in itself serve to reduce the potential biasing effects of the experimenter. For example, assume that the experimenter learns from the participants' responses how to influence them unintentionally. This learning takes time, and with fewer participants from whom to learn the unintentional communication system, the experimenter may learn less of the system.

Another advantage gained when each experimenter contacts fewer participants is related primarily to the method of blind contact (i.e., the experimenters are unaware of which participants are receiving the experimental and control treatments). The fewer the participants each experimenter contacts, the less chance of an unwitting breakdown of the blind procedure. This advantage also resembles the way random errors cancel out, in

Table 3.3

Strategies for the Control of Expectancy Effects

1. Increasing the number of experimenters

   - Decreases the learning of influence techniques.
   - Helps to maintain blindness (see also 4 below).
   - Randomizes expectancies.
   - Minimizes the effects of early data returns.
   - Increases the generality of the results.
   - Permits statistical correction (see also 3 below).

2. Monitoring the behavior of experimenters

   - Permits the correction of unprogrammed behavior.
   - Sometimes reduces expectancy effects.
   - Facilitates a greater standardization of experimenter behavior.

3. Statistical analysis

   - Permits inferences about changes in experimenter behavior.
   - Permits correction for expectancy effect.

4. Maintaining blind contact minimizes expectancy effects.

5. Minimizing experimenter-subject contact

   - Minimizes interactional effects.
   - Minimizes expectancy effects.

6. Using expectancy control groups permits assessment of expectancy effects.

that this procedure "randomizes" expectancies so that the experimenters' different expectancies will cancel one another if there are enough experimenters.

A further advantage of increasing the number of experimenters is that it will minimize the biasing effects of early data returns on later data returns. That is, when all the results of a study are "nearly in," there is less need for the experimenter to catch a glimpse of the early returns, and therefore less chance that these returns will have a biasing effect. Even beyond expectancy bias, increasing the number of experimenters may help to increase the generality of the results. We can be more confident of a result obtained by a larger number of experimenters than of a result obtained by only one experimenter.

Monitoring the behavior of the experimenters—the second strategy in Table 3.3—may not by itself eliminate expectancy bias, but it will help in identifying unprogrammed experimenter behaviors. If we make our observations during a preexperimental phase, we may be able to use this information to select good experimenters. The problem is that this selection procedure may be unintentionally biased, so it may be preferable simply to assign experimenters to experiments randomly. Nevertheless, monitoring may alleviate intentional error and perhaps some of the other biasing effects noted in the previous chapter, and it should facilitate greater standardization among the experimenters.

The third strategy is to use simple statistical analyses to look for changes in experimenter behavior from the first to the last set of participants. We can do a median split of the participants seen by each experimenter and compare the behavior of the participants in each half. Is the mean of the group the same? Is the amount of variability in performance of the participants the same in both halves? We may also be able to correct for expectancy effects. For example, in some cases, we will find expectancies distributed only dichotomously; either a result is expected or it is not. At other times, we will have an ordering of expectancies in terms of either ranks or absolute values. In any of these cases, we can correlate the results obtained by the experimenters with their expectancies. If the correlation is trivial in magnitude, we are reassured that expectancy effects were probably not operating. If the correlation is substantial, we conclude that expectancy effects did occur. These can then be "corrected" or at least analyzed by such statistical methods as partial correlation or blocking strategies.

The fourth strategy is based on the idea that, if the experimenter does not know whether the participant is in the experimental or the control group, then the experimenter can have no validly based expectancy about how the participant *should* respond. That is, the experimenter who is "blind" to the participants' treatment condition cannot be expected unintentionally to treat participants differentially as a function of their group membership. In drug trials, for example, in a *single-blind* study, the participants do not know the group or condition (e.g., drug vs. placebo) to which they have been randomly assigned. In a *double-blind* study, both the experimenters and the participants are kept from knowing what drug or treatment has been administered. Psychologists have been slow to adopt the double-blind method for other than drug trials, but when it is feasible, it is more than warranted to minimize the possibility of expectancy effects.

A problem, however, is that single-blind and double-blind methods are not very easy. In the single-blind method, although no investigator would tell the participants what their responses "ought" to be, cues from the situation (even if not from the experimenter) may unintentionally communicate to the participants how they are expected to behave. We will return to this point in the next chapter, but even in the case of double-blind experiments, the participant's conduct may give clues to the experimenter about what treatment the participant has received. In subsequent interactions, these clues may be a source of expectancy "side effects."

Imagine a study in which anxiety is the independent variable. People who have just been through an anxiety-arousing experience, or who have scored high on a test of anxiety, may behave in an identifiable way in an experimental situation. The "blind" experimenters may then covertly "diagnose" the level of anxiety. If they know the hypothesis, they may unwittingly bias the results of the experiment in the expected direction or, by bending over backward to avoid bias, "spoil" the study. There are many experimental treatments or measures that may be assessed unintentionally by the "blind" data collector. In one study, it was found that participants scoring high in need for social approval arrived earlier at the site of the experiment.[43] Arrival time, overt anxiety, and a score of other, more subtle signs may break down the most carefully arranged double-blind study.

A fifth strategy is to minimize the experimenter-participant contact, which may be much easier than to maintain blind contact. In the computer era, the day may come when the elimination of the experimenter, in person, will be a widespread, well-accepted practice. By computer, we can generate hypotheses, sample hypotheses, sample the experimental treatment conditions from a population of potential manipulations, select our participants randomly, invite their participation, schedule them, instruct them, record and analyze their responses, and even partially interpret and report the results. In experiments that *require* human interaction, it may be possible at least to minimize that contact. For example, using an ordinary tape recorder and a screen interposed between the experimenter and the participant may achieve some of the advantages of using a filmed experimenter to contact the participants.

Expectancy Control Design

The final strategy listed in Table 3.3 is the use of expectancy control groups. The beauty of this approach is that we can compare the effects of experimenter expectations with some other behavioral research variable. Table 3.4 shows the most basic expectancy control design, in which there are two row levels of the behavioral research variable and two column levels of the experimenter expectancy variable. Cell A represents the condition in which the experimental treatment is administered to the participants by a data collector who expects the occurrence of the treatment effect. Cell D represents the condition in which the absence of the experimental treatment is associated with a data collector who expects the nonoccurrence of the treatment effect.

But ordinarily, the investigator is interested in the treatment effects, unconfounded with experimenter expectancy. The addi-

Table 3.4

Basic Expectancy Control Design

| | Expectancy | |
Treatment condition	Occurrence	Nonoccurrence
Occurrence	A	B
Nonoccurrence	C	D

tion of the appropriate expectancy control groups permits the evaluation of the treatment separately from the expectancy effect. A *complete* expectancy control design requires the addition of Cells B *and* C, whereas a *partial* expectancy control design requires the addition of either B *or* C. The participants in Cell B receive the experimental treatment and are contacted by an experimenter who does not expect a treatment effect. The participants in Cell C do not receive the experimental treatment and are contacted by an experimenter who expects a treatment effect.

Table 3.5 shows the results of a study by J. R. Burnham that used a complete expectancy design.[44] He had 23 experimenters each run one rat in a T-maze discrimination problem. About half the rats had been lesioned by the removal of portions of the brain; the remaining animals had received only sham surgery, which involved cutting through the skull but no damage to the brain tissue. The purpose of the study was explained to the experimenters as an attempt to learn the effects of lesions on discrimination learning. Expectancies were manipulated by labeling each rat as lesioned or unlesioned. Some of the really lesioned rats were labeled accurately as "lesioned" (Cell A), and some were falsely labeled as "unlesioned" (Cell B). Some of the unle-

Table 3.5

Expectancy Control Design Used by Burnham to Study Discrimination Learning in Rats as a Function of Brain Lesions and Experimenter Expectancies

	Expectancy		
Brain state	"Lesioned"	"Nonlesioned"	Sum
Lesioned	46.5	49.0	95.5
Nonlesioned	48.2	58.3	106.5
Sum	94.7	107.3	

sioned rats were labeled accurately as "unlesioned" (Cell D), and some were falsely labeled as "lesioned" (Cell C).

The table shows the standard scores of the ranks of performance in each of the four conditions (higher scores denote superior performance). Animals that had been lesioned did not perform as well as those that had not been lesioned. Animals that were believed to be lesioned did not perform as well as those that were believed to be unlesioned. What makes this experiment of special interest is that the effects of expectancy ($d = 1.02$; $r = .45$) were somewhat larger than those of the actual removal of brain tissue ($d = 0.79$; $r = .37$). It emphasizes the value of separating expectancy effects from the effects of the independent variable of interest, to avoid misrepresenting the impact of either variable.

Chapter 4

The Person Behind the Look

The fact that the experimenter controls the information available to the subject and that he never reveals completely what he is trying to discover and how he will judge what he observes—this feature gives the experiment much of its character as a game or contest. It leads to a set of inferential and interpretive activities on the part of the subject in an effort to penetrate the experimenter's inscrutability and to arrive at some conception of the meaning that the unrevealed categories of response have for the latter.

—Henry W. Riecken[1]

Demand Characteristics

There is an old saying that it takes two to tango; it also applies to the experimenter-participant partnership that leads to certain interactional artifacts, as discussed in the previous chapters. So far, we have concentrated on the experimenter in this relationship, and we now shift our attention to the other partner in order to get an insight into, as Riecken stated, the participants' "inferential and interpretive activities." An analogy suggested by the philosopher Jean-Paul Sartre helps to underscore the idea that we need to look behind a participant's behavior to catch a glimpse of the interpretive agent who serves as our model of people in general.[2] As Sartre put it, when we observe someone who is looking back at us, it is hard for us to apprehend the "watcher" behind the "look" at the same time that we focus on the person's appearance. The more we stare only at what is overt, the less likely we are to perceive the sentient and active person behind the look. The "person" is neutralized, put out of play, by a human consciousness requiring that certain elements be disconnected. To glimpse the whole person, we shift our concentration back and forth, attending first to behavior and then to motivation.

Shifting our attention to motives that may impel a research participant to behave in a particular way, we begin by reviewing the pioneering work of Martin T. Orne. Simultaneously with the first investigations of expectancy bias, Orne made an important discovery in his work on artifacts that are associated with the participants' motives and experimental behavior. He noted that, at the conclusion of many of his experiments, the participants often asked questions such as "Did I ruin the study?" After postexperimental interviews with his participants, Orne deduced that what they had meant was "Did I perform well in my role as experimental subject?" or "Did my behavior demonstrate what the study was designed to show?"[3] He argued that the participants had been responding to what they interpreted to be task-orienting cues about what the experiment was "really" about and what the experimenter "wanted" to find.

Borrowing a concept (*Aufforderungscharakter*) from the work of Kurt Lewin,[4] one of the founders of modern social psychology, Orne called the cues that governed people's perceptions of the purpose of an experiment the *demand characteristics of the experimental situation*. In a series of ingenious studies, Orne and his coworkers at the University of Pennsylvania demonstrated how demand characteristics can influence research participants' behaviors to produce both artifacts and spurious conclusions. He also developed the idea of using so-called quasi controls to identify the demand cues of an experimental situation. Some leading social psychologists disagreed with Orne about the particular motivations of research participants; we will examine their alternative interpretations as well. And finally, we will describe a conceptual model that pulls together the various theoretical threads and provides a template for control strategies.

The "Good Subject" Effect

Orne was primarily interested in the nature of hypnosis when he began his program of investigation, and three explanations of hypnosis occurred to him as hypotheses to be tested.[5] What we all know as the phenomenon of hypnosis might, he theorized, be the result of (1) people's preconceptions and related behavior; (2) people's responses to inadvertent cues given by hypnotists; or (3) the particular techniques of trance induction. Orne's experiments to assess these alternative hypotheses led him to posit that what basically produces the trance manifestations a person shows on entering hypnosis is the individual's motivation to "act out" the role of a hypnotized subject. Both the person's preconceptions of how a hypnotized subject ought to act and the cues communicated by the hypnotist are, Orne posited, determinants of the person's expectations concerning how this role is to be enacted.

Orne first gathered empirical support for this interpretation using students in an introductory psychology course as participants.[6] In two sections of the course, a demonstration of hypnosis was carried out on several participants. The demonstration participants in one section were given the suggestion that, on entering a hypnotic trance, they would manifest "catalepsy of the dominant hand." All the students in this section were told that catalepsy of the dominant hand was a standard reaction of the hypnotized person, and the class's attention was called to the fact that the right-handed person had catalepsy of the right hand and the left-handed person had catalepsy of the left hand. In the other section, the demonstration of hypnosis was carried out, but without the display of Orne's concocted symptom of "catalepsy."

In the next phase of this study, Orne asked for volunteers for hypnosis from each section and had them tested in such a way that the experimenter could not tell which lecture they had attended until after the completion of the experiment. Of the nine volunteers from the first section, five showed catalepsy of the dominant hand, two showed catalepsy of both hands, and two showed no catalepsy. None of the volunteers in the control section showed catalepsy of the dominant hand, but three of them showed catalepsy of both hands. Because catalepsy of the dominant hand (the symptom *invented* by Orne) was known not to occur spontaneously, its occurrence in the first group but not in the second could be seen as providing confirmatory evidence for Orne's hypothesis that "trance behavior" is affected by the person's preconceptions of the hypnotic state. That three of nine volunteers in the control group spontaneously displayed catalepsy of both hands was explained by Orne in terms of the experimenters' repeated testing for catalepsy, which he viewed as an implicit source of task-orienting cues.

Orne referred to the remarkably cooperative behavior of the volunteer participants in the experimental condition as "the good subject effect," and he noted that the "good subject" goes to remarkable lengths to comply with demand characteristics. Concerned that the good subject effect might be a source of confounding in his hypnosis research, Orne tried to devise dull, meaningless tasks that nonhypnotized participants would refuse to do or would try for only a short time and then abandon. One task consisted of adding hundreds of thousands of two-digit numbers. Five and a half hours after the participants began, Orne gave up! Even when they were told to tear each worksheet into a minimum of 32 pieces before going on to the next, they persisted. Orne explained this behavior as the "role enactment" of individuals who reasoned that, no matter how trivial and inane the assigned task seemed to them, it must surely have some important scientific purpose or they would not have been asked to participate in the first place. Thus, Orne argued, they complied with the demand characteristics of the experiment in order to "further the cause of science."[7]

Orne got another insight into this situation when he asked a number of casual acquaintances to do an experimenter a favor and, on their acquiescence, asked them to do five push-ups. They seemed amazed and incredulous, and all simply responded "Why?" However, when he asked a similar group of individuals whether they would take part in a brief experiment and, on their acquiescence, asked them to do five push-ups, their typical response was "Where?"[8] What could account for the dramatic difference in responses? Orne theorized that people who volunteer to participate in experiments implicitly agree to comply with whatever demand cues seem inherent in the experimental situation. Research participants are concerned about the outcome of the experiment in which they have agreed to participate. Consequently, they are often motivated to play the role of the good subject who responds to overt and implicit cues in ways designed to validate the experimenter's hypothesis. The good subject complies "altruistically" with the request to do five push-ups thinking that, no matter how unpleasant or trivial the task, it must have some important scientific purpose.

Research by other investigators implies similar effects of compliance with demand cues. Irwin Silverman randomly assigned college students to four groups that read a 250-word argument in favor of using closed-circuit television tapes to give lectures to large classes. The students were more easily persuaded when told they were "subjects in an experiment" than if this information was not communicated to them; they were also more easily persuaded when they had to sign their opinions than when they were tested anonymously.[9] Another researcher manipulated demand cues in a figure-ground perception experiment and found that the participants, particularly those with some elementary knowledge of psychology, responded in ways they were led to believe the experimenter wanted.[10] Other studies imply the existence of uncontrolled, biasing demand cues in prisoners' dilemma games,[11] attitude change research,[12] verbal operant conditioning,[13] classical conditioning,[14] autokinetic effect research,[15] hypnosis and sensory deprivation,[16] perceptual defense,[17] psychophysics,[18] test taking,[19] evaluations of therapy,[20] autonomic activity,[21] and small-group research on leadership and conformity.[22]

Evaluation Apprehension

Other social psychologists interested in participant-related artifacts have proposed different ideas about the motives of typical participants. Riecken suggested that one of the important motives of the research participant is to "look good,"[23] and a similar idea was later advanced by Milton J. Rosenberg. Rosenberg ran a series of experiments to demonstrate the biasing effects of an anxiety-toned state he termed *evaluation apprehension*. He said that typical participants approached the psychology experiment anticipating that the experimenter would evaluate their psychological competence. Not surprisingly, most participants became apprehensive about being evaluated negatively (or at least not positively), and they developed their own hypotheses about how to win approval and to avoid disapproval. Experienced experimenters who bothered to talk to their participants had all heard questions like these: "How did I do—were my responses (answers) normal?" "What were you really trying to find out, whether I'm some kind of neurotic?" "Did I react the same as most people do?"[24] Such questions imply the presence of evaluation anxiety, Rosenberg argued.

Rosenberg's experiments uncovered some of the circumstances in which evaluation apprehension is likely to occur. These circumstances include experiments that contain an element of surprise or have an aura of mystery about them—which was typical of many social psychology experiments in the 1960s. Rosenberg found that the more feedback participants got about the quality of their performance, the more error resulted, as the participants guided their performance in whatever direction seemed to produce a favorable evaluation. The more explicit the cues, the more control the experimenter had in granting positive evaluation, or the less effortful the participant's responses, the greater was the resulting error due to evaluation apprehension.

In his most famous study, Rosenberg went head to head with the most prominent and controversial sociopsychological theory of that decade: Leon Festinger's cognitive dissonance theory.[25] Dissonance theory had, like the artifact research, stimulated an enormous amount of discussion. There was also a controversy brewing about the validity of its premises and assertions.[26] In a paper published in 1965, Rosenberg developed the argument that some experimental procedures used by dissonance researchers had unwittingly produced artifacts.[27] Their procedures, he argued, had aroused feelings of evaluation apprehension, not cognitive dissonance. In effect, the results had been due to the participants' motivation to behave in a way that would not lead to an unfavorable evaluation, Rosenberg contended. Several attempts were made to reconcile Rosenberg's position with the dissonance theorists' position,[28] but by this time, there was a barrage of papers implying all sorts of artifacts.[29]

The Obedient Subject

Besides Orne's idea of the altruistic person who wants to help the cause of science and Rosenberg's notion of the person who only wants to look good, some other ideas were proposed. Another viable candidate to explain the motives of typical participants came out of a famous debate and controversy between Orne and Stanley Milgram. In a series of experiments, Milgram had studied how far a research participant will go in subjecting someone else to pain at the order of an authority figure.[30] Milgram told how he had come up with the idea for his studies as a way to make a set of classic studies by Solomon Asch "more humanly significant."[31] Milgram was particularly interested in obedience to authority, however, because of his profound dismay about the horrifying effects of blind obedience to Nazi commands in World War II. In his research, Milgram tricked volunteer participants placed in the role of the "teacher" into believing they would be giving varying degrees of painful electric shock to a third person (the "learner") each time the learner made a mistake in a certain task. Milgram varied the distance between the teacher and the learner, to see whether the teacher would be less ruthless in administering the electric shocks as he or she got closer and the learner pressed the teacher to quit.

To Milgram, as well as to a great many others, his findings were almost beyond belief. Many participants (the "teachers") unhesitatingly obeyed the experimenter's "Please continue" or "You have no choice, you must go on" and continued to increase the level of the shocks no matter how much the learner pleaded with the "teacher" to stop. What especially surprised Milgram was that no participant ever walked out of the laboratory in disgust or protest. This remarkable obedience occurred time and time again in several universities where the experiment was repeated. Milgram stated, "It is the extreme willingness of adults to go to almost any lengths on the command of an authority that constitutes the chief finding of the study and the fact most urgently demanding explanation."[32]

Although the "learner" in these studies was a confederate of Milgram's and no actual shocks were transmitted by the "teacher," concerns about ethics and values arose and have dogged these studies ever since they were first reported. We will refer to this study again, but more pertinent here is that an article by Milgram reprinted in the *American Journal of Psychiatry* was followed by a critique by Orne and Charles Holland. They used a demand characteristics analysis to deconstruct the obedience research. Milgram was invited to give a colloquium at the University of Pennsylvania; he proposed that it be in the form of a debate between himself and Orne. The auditorium was filled to capacity, and one of us was fortunate to be in the audience. Orne argued that Milgram's "technical illusion" (Milgram's term for his experimental paradigm) would merely have been seen by his participants as resembling a magician's illusion—a "scientific practical joke."

In their earlier written critique, Orne and Holland had argued that Milgram's participants behaved in the same way volunteers in hypnosis experiments behaved. Orne and Holland gave an anecdotal illustration, reaching back to 1889, in which

> a deeply hypnotized patient stabbed individuals with rubber daggers, poisoned their tea with sugar, and carried out any other type of murder or mayhem required of her. This demonstration was very impressive, and after the distinguished guests had left, the [patient] was left to be awakened by students who wished to end the experiment on a lighter note. They suggested to the patient that she was alone, about to take a bath, and should undress. Her response to the suggestion was to awaken immediately, greatly disturbed. It is one thing to "kill" people during an experimental situation with means that cannot really do damage; it is quite another to be asked to undress in a context that transcends the experimental situation.[33]

In Orne and Holland's anecdote, the patient was responding to demand cues, and they argued that the participants in Milgram's obedience experiments were also doing so. His instructions to the participants that they "must go on," and the "learner's" shouts of chest pain were interpreted by Orne and Holland as making the paradigm no different "from the stage magician's trick where a volunteer from the audience is strapped into the guillotine and another volunteer is required to trip the release lever."[34] Milgram, of course, vehemently defended the validity of his paradigm and replied to Orne and Holland's critique point by point.[35] He referred to a film of his experiment (still available) in which, he said, people could see for themselves the sincerity and obedience of his participants. He disputed Orne's vision of typical participants as being deliberative, skeptical, and problem solving. Milgram said that participants are accepting and compliant (obedient) in the face of authority. Out of this argument grew the idea that typical subjects in psychology experiments might be playing the role of a "faithful subject."

The Dayyan's Decree

Persuasive arguments were made favoring one or another motivational basis of the participants' experimental behavior, yet it also seemed plausible that Orne, Milgram, and Rosenberg might *all* be right to some extent. The situation was reminiscent of an old Yiddish anecdote about a rabbinical judge, or dayyan, who was asked by a married couple to mediate a disagreement. The wife told her side and the dayyan said, "You are right." The husband then told his side and the dayyan responded, "You are right." An incredulous student who overheard the conversations addressed the dayyan: "Rebbe, you told them they were both right, but surely they both can't be a hundred percent right." The dayyan replied, "You are right, too."[36] Many years ago, Donald T. Campbell and Julian C. Stanley cautioned behavioral researchers that, "when one finds, for example, that competent observers advocate strongly divergent points of view, it seems likely on a priori grounds that both have observed something valid about the natural situation, and that both represent a part of the truth."[37] Of course, universal agreement is no certain adjudication of truth, which in science also relies on empirical confrontation.

Subsequent research seems to imply that Orne, Milgram, and Rosenberg had each seized on a part of the truth, and that all were right to some extent. One aspect of this research has simply asked some typical prospective participants to project how they perceived the role of the research subject. Many years earlier, Quinn McNemar had said, "The existing science of human behavior is largely the science of the behavior of sophomores."[38] He was referring to the fact that undergraduate students taking introductory psychology were overrepresented as participants because of their availability. The results of several surveys (noted in Table 4.1) later confirmed McNemar's conclusion. The surveys showed the percentages of research participants as ranging from 70% to 90% college students, with a median of 80%. A later survey reported that college students

Table 4.1

College Students as a Percentage of Total Subjects Used

Source	Years	% College students
Journal of Abnormal and Social Psychology[a]	1962–64	73
Journal of Experimental Psychology[a]	1963–64	86
Journal of Personality and Social Psychology[b]	1966–67	70
Journal of Experimental Psychology[b]	1966–67	84
Psychology department survey[c]	1967–68	90
Journal of Personality and Social Psychology[d]	1969	76

[a]R. G. Smart, "Subject Selection Bias in Psychological Research," *Canadian Psychologist,* 1966, vol. 7a, 115–121.
[b]D. P. Schultz, "The Human Subject in Psychological Research," *Psychological Bulletin,* 1969, vol. 72, pp. 214–228.
[c]J. Jung, "Current Practices and Problems in the Use of College Students for Psychological Research," *Canadian Psychologist,* 1969, vol. 10, pp. 280–290.
[d]K. L. Higbee and M. G. Wells, "Some Research Trends in Social Psychology during the 1960s," *American Psychologist,* 1972, vol. 27, pp. 963–966.

continued to be a favored population of behavioral researchers even into the 1980s.[39]

Concerns about the use of students as the model of "persons in general" were based not only on the very obvious differences between college students and more representative persons in age, intelligence, and social class, but also on the suspicion that college students, because of their special relationship with the teacher-investigator, may be especially sensitive and responsive to demand cues. Silverman compared this situation, in which researchers struggled to find out what participants *really* felt and thought about playing the role of a "research subject" in an experiment, to the fable of the Emperor's clothes:

A student and seasoned subject once said to me, with apparent innocence: "If everyone does things in experiments for the same reasons I do, I don't understand how you can find out anything that's true." I liken her to the child in the fable, to whom we may now say: "Yes, the Emperor is naked."[40]

To get a further insight into this problem, a scaling study was designed by Rosnow and Leona S. Aiken[41] in which typical participants were asked to compare the role of "research subject" with certain everyday situations that seemed to reflect the hypotheses advanced by Orne, Rosenberg, and Milgram. Orne had argued that participants respond to task-orienting cues because they hope and expect "the study in which they are participating will in some material way contribute to human welfare in general":[42] two everyday situations that reflect a similar "altruistic" motivation are giving anonymously to charity and working free as a lab assistant. Milgram's hypothesis about an "obedient subject" had been fleshed out to imply "dutifully going along with the instructions,"[43] and a team of researchers stated, "Subjects are obedient in the sense that if they are instructed to do something, they fulfill that request";[44] two everyday situations that reflect this idea are obeying a no-smoking sign and not arguing with the professor. Rosenberg's hypothesis was that typical participants approach the typical psychology experiment expecting to be evaluated on some basic psychological dimension; some familiar situations tapping into "evaluation anxieties" are taking a final exam and being interviewed for a job.

In the Rosnow and Aiken study, all these situations were paired with one another and with four positive and negative anchoring situations. Psychology students in an introductory class (typical participants) were instructed to project their own impressions simply by rating each pair of situations using a 15-point scale from maximum dissimilarity (1) to maximum similarity (15). The scaling results are shown in Figure 4.1.[45] One dimension was inferred to be work-oriented, and the other dimension, affective.

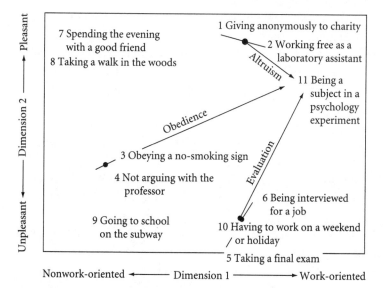

Figure 4.1. A two-dimensional scaling solution based on the individual judgments of 88 subjects. The lines labeled "Altruism," "Evaluation," and "Obedience" reflect the relative distances between these three factors and the target situation ("being a subject in a psychology experiment"). The proximity of any pair of situations indicates the judged similarity in role expectations for the pair members.

The proximity of situations in this figure reflects how close a situation was to another situation in the students' ratings. We see that the two situations reflecting Orne's altruistic role are the closest to "being a subject in a psychology experiment," but being obedient and being apprehensive are also part of the picture in these students' responses. We also note that research participation was not perceived as unpleasant and was perceived as work-oriented.

In another study by Aiken and Rosnow (with the assistance of Susan M. Anthony and Marianne E. Jaeger), 374 high school boys and girls were given a questionnaire that explored their ideas about the role of "human subject."[46] Orne had stated, "Most volunteer subjects participating in a psychological experiment recognize it as an elaborate ritual with rules that are reasonably well understood by them as well as by most experimenters."[47] This population of high school students had never participated in a psychology study, and none of them could recall ever having been asked to do so. Thus their responses were expected to reveal how deeply ingrained the good subject stereotype is. They were asked, "How do you think the typical human subject is expected to behave in a psychology experiment?" They answered by circling characteristics on a long list of positive and negative attributes. Both boys and girls made similar choices ($r = .90$); both sexes described the typical participant as cooperative, alert, observant, good-tempered, frank, helpful, logical, and trustful. This stereotype is, in some respects, reminiscent of Orne's and Milgram's ideas: typical participants' experimental behavior resembles that of the proverbial Boy Scout who makes a habit of being cooperative, alert, observant, helpful, and so on; if he has not helped any little old ladies across the street lately, it may be that no authority has asked him to.[48]

Findings such as these allow us to look behind the research participant's behavior, and they imply what our prospective participants may be thinking when they reflect on the role of "research subject." The findings do not tell us whether people behave accordingly when the opportunity arises to enact this role. Suppose there were a conflict between the cues associated with evaluation apprehension and those associated with cooperation. How would participants caught in such a conflict respond? This question was first experimentally addressed by Harold Sigall, Elliot Aronson, and Thomas Van Hoose, who designed a complicated deception study in which two sets of cues occurred simultaneously in one of the treatment conditions.[49] One set of cues involved the demand characteristics of the experiment, and the second set conveyed the idea that complying with these demand characteristics would result in the respondent's being unfavorably evaluated on an important psychological dimension. Instead of responding altruistically, the participants responded in the direction of promoting a favorable self-image.

This research led to a number of follow-up studies, in which the researchers either challenged Sigall et al.'s results or each other's findings. For example, John Adair and B. S. Schachter argued that Sigall et al.'s research finding was itself subject to an artifact interpretation.[50] In a modified replication of Sigall et al.'s study, Adair and Schachter found that people's responses to demand cues superseded their responses to evaluative cues. In another follow-up study, these findings were challenged by another team of researchers, who showed that research participants opted to "look good" rather than to "help the cause of science" when faced with a conflict between these two choices.[51] The collective results in this area suggest, as implied by the dayyan's decree, that multiple motivations may be operating and that each may account for a part of the truth. Other findings in psychology have raised the possibility that personality[52] and situational variables affect how the role of "research subject" will be enacted in a particular research setting.[53]

Mediation of Participant-Related Artifacts

Back in the 1970s, some researchers expressed their feeling of being overwhelmed by artifacts. Someone once compared this situation with trying to balance dozens of spinning plates on the ends of sticks. One has to keep running back and forth to keep them all balanced, just as researchers felt they had to concentrate on one source of artifacts after another in order to keep everything properly balanced. What was needed, it seemed, was a conceptual pulling together of what was known about participant-related artifacts within the framework of a simple, comprehensive model. Such a model has evolved in a collaboration by Rosnow successively with Leona Aiken, Daniel J. Davis, and David Strohmetz.[54] Instead of focusing on specific artifact-producing variables, this model concentrates on three intervening (or mediational) steps in the theorized causal chain from demand cues to artifacts.

The latest representation of the model is shown in Figure 4.2, where the three intervening steps are denoted as the research participant's (1) *receptivity* of task-orienting cues (demand characteristics); (2) *motivation* to comply with such cues; and (3) *capability* of complying with such cues.[55] If, as shown in this figure, the answer is yes to all three mediational questions, then the participant's experimental behavior is held suspect. In other words, for demand cues to have a biasing effect on behavior in an experiment, such cues must be received, and the participant must be motivated and able to respond to them. Thus, if participants are unaware of demand cues, or are not motivated to respond to them, or are incapable of responding to them, the experimental behavior at the end of this chain is "unadulterated" by artifacts.[56]

This model helps us piece together what we know about causes of participant-related artifacts and serves as a template for control strategies. We know, for example, that ideas about the purpose of a study (demand cues) can originate in rumors, campus scuttlebutt, information given in lectures, and preliminary information presented to the participants by the experimenter. Although participants may have prior knowledge of the purpose of the experiment and may think they know how they are expected to behave, many of them will still be apprehensive and uncertain about what behaviors are actually expected of them.[57] As Riecken and Orne argued, participants frequently engage in problem solving to discover how they should behave. To initiate this problem solving, then, what is needed are cues that may provide the participants with ideas about what the experimenter wants of them.[58]

The next link in this chain is for the participant to receive these cues. That is, in order for demand cues to influence participants' behaviors, resulting in an artifact, the participants must have an inkling of what is expected of them. If the participants are unaware of task-orienting cues suggesting how they should

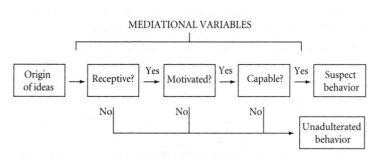

MEDIATIONAL VARIABLES

Figure 4.2. The mediation of participant-related artifacts.

respond to the experimental stimuli, then we have increased confidence that their responses to the stimuli have been unaffected by such cues. If the demand cues in the experimental situation are strong and salient, then we must have suspicions about whether the participants were responding to the independent variable of interest, the demand cues, or a combination of both.

There seem to be two main sources of such cues in virtually every experimental situation: the experimental design and the experimenter. Lana studied the problem of using a design with before and after measures (a pretest-posttest design) instead of a design that takes measures only after the treatment (an after-only design). He found that sometimes participants found demand cues merely in the fact that before and after measures of the same variable were taken. That is, a pretest-posttest design may communicate that some change in behavior is desired or expected.[59] In the case of a learning experiment, the expectation communicated is that the participant should pay special attention to the experimental stimuli because evidence of learning is sought by the experimenter. Previously, we discussed how the experimenter himself or herself can also be an inadvertent source of demand cues in a study.

The third link in this model of the artifact chain is the participants' motivations in the experiment. Even if they are aware of demand cues, whether they use this information may depend on their reasons for participating in the study. That is, if a participant is receptive to demand cues but is not motivated to act in accordance with them (and is also not motivated to impair the results purposely), then his or her response to the experimental stimuli will be unaffected by the demand cues. However, if the person is not only aware of the demand cues but is also motivated to act on them, the likelihood is increased that the experimental outcome will be distorted by artifacts.

What types of motivation might lead a participant to be compliant or noncompliant? Orne suggested that, frequently, people enter into an experiment because they want to help the cause of science, and he showed that research participants are remarkably willing to perform a wide range of acts with extraordinary diligence. In the next chapter, we will discuss how volunteers for research participation are especially apt to play the good subject role described by Orne, but this role does not rule out those other roles described by Rosenberg and Milgram.

The fourth link in the artifact chain is each participant's ability to respond to the demand cues perceived in the experimental situation. People who volunteer to participate are often highly receptive and sensitive to such cues and are also highly motivated to respond to them, but artifacts are not introduced if the participants are unable to act on their receptivity and motivation. For example, in an attitude change experiment using a before-after design, suppose the participants' responses on the pretest were so extreme that they were unable to move any further in that direction on the posttest. In that case, the demand cues would have little impact on how participants actually respond in the experiment. However, of the three mediators—receptivity, motivation, and capability—capability may have the least impact on whether the participants' responses to the independent variable should be viewed as either "suspect" or "unadulterated." The reason is that not many experimenters would design a study so that the participants would be *incapable* of responding to cues closely tied to the experimenters' own expectations.

Table 4.2

Strategies for Minimizing Experimental Artifacts

Receptivity manipulations to minimize demand clarity

1. Measure the dependent variable in a setting not obviously connected with the treatment, or employ unobtrusive measurements.

2. Measure the dependent variable removed in time from the treatment.

3. Use an after-only rather than a before-after design, especially in attitude change experiments. If a before-after design seems to be essential, use control groups to tease out pretest-sensitization bias.

4. Standardize and restrict the experimenter's communication with the subjects.

5. Use "blind" procedures in testing and experimental manipulations.

Receptivity manipulation to generate alternate demands

6. If it can be fully justified on scientific and ethical grounds, use a deception strategy that elicits false hypotheses about the purpose of the study.

Motivational manipulations to encourage honest responding

7. Give feedback of overly compliant behavior in a set of preexperimental tasks in order to bring the subject to a state of "nonacquiescence" to demand cues in later trials.

8. Make the experimental setting and procedures nonthreatening and low-keyed; in particular, ensure subject anonymity, or at least use confidential responding procedures.

The final link in Figure 4.2 is the behavioral outcome and whether participant-related artifacts are probable. If it can be assumed that the participants were not only receptive to demand cues but were also motivated to comply with them and quite capable of compliance, then the suspicion of artifacts is justifiably raised. Alternatively, if it can be argued that there was a break in the artifact chain, it can be further argued that the participants' responses were really a result of the independent variable of interest.

Minimizing Experimental Artifacts

We turn now to strategies for coping with participant-related artifacts, which Table 4.2 summarizes within the framework of the mediational model. If we accept the logic of this model, then the control or elimination of such artifacts depends on a disruption of the chain of variables in Figure 4.2.

First, if participants are unaware they are participating in a study, they will not be looking for demand cues. For example, Bruce Rind was interested in how awareness of weather, which is one of the most pervasive background environmental variables in human life, bears on ordinary behavior.[60] In one study, conducted in an Atlantic City casino behind dark-tinted windows, he had a room-service waiter randomly inform guests that it was warm and sunny, warm and rainy, or cold and rainy. The dependent measure was not obviously connected to the disguised manipulation, as it was meant to be an unobtrusive variable: tipping behavior. The results were that guests tipped an average 29% of the bill when told it was sunny, 24% when cloudy, and 19% when rainy. It may not be easy to get a study of this nature approved by a review board because of the proposed use of deception, although Rind's ideas were approved before he ran the study. Social psychologists who do these disguised experiments using unobtrusive measures argue that the people studied are treated confidentially and that the risks of the mild deceptions are no greater than any risks in everyday life.[61]

Second, the close pairing of the treatment and the measurement frequently enhances receptivity by sensitizing the participants to demand cues. Because these cues are often transmitted by the relationship between the treatment and the measurement, the separation of these two processes in space and time may reduce demand clarity and may also lower the probability of receptivity. For example, one researcher can run the experiment, and another researcher can administer the measures, preferably elsewhere and at another time.

Third, we alluded to the confounding effects in pretest-posttest designs. Lana noted that these are not always a problem,[62] but they do seem to surface in certain kinds of psychological and educational studies. For example, Richard L. Solomon pretested several groups of children on a list of words of equal difficulty by having the children spell the words. The children were then given a lesson on the rules of correct spelling and afterward were tested on the same list of words. The results showed that taking the pretest made the children more resistant to the spelling lesson (called *pretest sensitization bias*).[63] In another study, Doris R. Entwisle investigated her participants' ability to learn the state locations of large U.S. cities. Her results suggested that pretest sensitization had aided the recall of high-IQ people and was mildly hindering to average-IQ people.[64] The use of designs without pretests, or the use of a special design developed by Solomon to control for pretest sensitization bias (described in the next chapter),[65] is another coping strategy.

Fourth, as elaborated in Chapter 3, researchers are usually the main channel for communicating cues concerning the purpose of the study and the participant's role. Among the coping strategies discussed in that chapter were standardizing and restricting the communication between the experimenter and the participants. Because even the experimenter's unconscious behavior can provide uncontrolled cues concerning the research hypotheses and expectations, the use of computers to present the experimental instructions (and possibly even manipulations of the variable of interest) should prevent this kind of bias.

There are other problems inherent in this mechanization of experiments. One potential limitation is that the mechanical manipulation may have little resemblance to the real-world phenomenon that the experimenter is attempting to study. It is also sometimes impossible to keep participants totally shielded from contact with the experimenters. In arranging an appointment, people connected with the study or the institution talk to the participants. Even saying "I can't tell you anything more" is bound to raise speculations in the participants' minds. Given these limitations, a fifth strategy for minimizing receptivity to demand cues unintentionally given by experimenters is to use "blind" experimenters. As described earlier, the experimenters are kept unaware of which participants are in the experimental and the control conditions. As noted in Chapter 3, more methodological leeway is possible if there are many experimenters who each work with only a few participants.

The sixth strategy is to create alternative demand cues. Here, the idea is to replace the true experimental cues with irrelevant task-orienting cues, and to make these irrelevant cues more salient to the participants than the true cues. This method has typically involved the use of mild deception procedures that create a new set of irrelevant cues. Once again, there are questions of research ethics to be addressed. Repeatedly using deception is bound to create the impression that "psychologists always lie." Such an impression may begin to define the rules of the game in a way that elicits hostility and dishonest responses because participants feel abused and morally outraged—concerns also previously recognized by Orne.[66]

Seventh, even when the participants are receptive to demand cues, the chain leading to suspect behavior can be broken by reducing their motivation to respond to such cues. For example, an experiment by Gustafson and Orne implied that focusing the participants' awareness on the fact that they were complying with demand cues in one task reduced their motivation to comply with demand cues in later trials.[67] In theory, studies could be preceded by procedures designed to bring the participants to a state of "noncompliance" with regard to demand cues only.

The eighth motivational strategy is to make the setting and procedures as low-keyed and nonthreatening as possible, so as not to arouse evaluation anxieties. For example, the mere asking of sensitive questions may make the respondents want to protect their privacy and withhold information about unacceptable behavior or, if they answer at all, to distort their responses in a socially desirable direction. Research suggests that ensuring the respondent's anonymity or confidentiality, inasmuch as it protects the person's privacy, can control evasive-answer bias.[68]

Detecting the Occurrence of Artifacts

The various strategies in Table 4.2 are a sample of the methods that have been proposed for circumventing or minimizing participant-related artifacts. An intriguing social psychological alternative, called the *bogus pipeline* by Edward E. Jones and Harold Sigall, uses a deception to promote honest disclosures by participants.[69] They are tricked into thinking that any dishonest responding on their part can be detected by a "physiological monitoring device" (actually a fake device) to which the participant is attached. If people naively accept that this device really can catch liars, they may respond more candidly to avoid being branded liars. Jones and Sigall, among others, have provided evidence that participants hooked up to the bogus pipeline tend to be more open and forthcoming when questioned about sensitive issues. Although this procedure has been used in the past, it is rather unlikely that, given current ethical sensitivities, it would be approved by an ethics review committee.

Other strategies for coping with artifacts have also been discussed, including trying to eliminate demand cues by traditional methods of control and making statistical adjustments. Orne's position was that demand characteristics "cannot be controlled in the classic sense" and should instead be thought of as "phenomena in their own right."[70] If demand cues are part and parcel of virtually all experiments, we may be limited to trying to detect such cues and then adjusting our conclusions accordingly. To help us decide whether our studies have been compromised by demand cues, we can use what Orne called quasi-control participants.[71] These are individuals who step out of the traditional participant role and act as coinvestigators in the search for truth. They help us identify the presence of certain artifacts by reflecting on the experiment and suggesting how their own behavior might be compromised or influenced by uncontrolled factors rather than by the controlled independent variable.

One procedure suggested by Orne is to use participants who serve as their own quasi controls through postexperimental interviews. In these interviews, the participants identify the factors that seemed important in determining their reactions in the experiment and also reveal their beliefs about and perceptions of the experiment and the experimenter. Care must be taken so that the demand cues operating during the experiment are not also operating during these postexperimental interviews. The quasi controls must be convinced that the "study is over" and that they are now to play the role of coinvestigators (or aides) in the search for knowledge.

Another quasi-control procedure suggested by Orne, called preinquiry, involves asking some prospective participants to imagine that they are real participants in the planned experiment. After being given a detailed description of what would happen to them during the experiment, they are asked to predict how they would behave in the experiment. Comparisons are made between their projected role responses and the actual responses made by real participants in the experiment. Any similarity between these two groups of responses suggests that the experimental outcome *may* have been affected by the real participants' guesses and role responses concerning how they should behave, rather than by the independent variable of interest. Orne used this strategy in his research on hypnosis as a way of detecting whether the trancelike behavior of hypnotized persons was merely conscious roleplaying.

A third quasi-control method noted by Orne uses "sacrificed" participants. In this case, the participation of some people is terminated ("sacrificed") at particular stages of the study, and these individuals are questioned about their perceptions of the experiment up to that point. The purpose of this strategy is to discover at what point uncontrolled factors may have compromised reactions in the experiment. This strategy, like the first one above, requires that the person "sacrificed" be willing to step out of the "subject role" and become a coinvestigator. It is recommended that the person be interviewed by someone distinctly apart from the study, who can convince the participant that the study is now over for this participant.

Another way of ferreting out participant-related artifacts, reminiscent of one aspect of the first strategy in Table 4.2, is to observe the dependent variable in several different settings.[72] A hypnosis study by Orne, Sheehan, and Evans illustrates this approach.[73] The hypnotized participants and a control group of volunteers who simulated being hypnotized were given the suggestion that, for the next 48 hours, every time they heard the word *experiment* mentioned, they would respond by running a hand over their head. This suggestion was tested in the original setting by having each person sign a receipt for payment received for participating in the "experiment." The next day, the participant was greeted by the researcher, who remarked, "I appreciate your making today's experiment." The participant was then met by the receptionist, who asked which "experiment" the person had reported for that day. In this way, it was possible to measure the critical response both outside and inside the experimental setting. The hypnotized participants tended to respond to the posthypnotic suggestion outside the research setting, but the simulators did not respond. These results were interpreted by Orne and his associates as indicating that posthypnotic behavior was not limited to the experimental setting. Such a strategy helps us see the subtle ways in which uncontrolled cues may operate in a particular setting.

Chapter 5

The Volunteer Subject

For the volunteer subject to feel that he has made a useful contribution, it is necessary for him to assume that the experimenter is competent and that he himself is a "good subject." . . . Viewed in this way, the student volunteer is not merely a passive responder in an experimental situation but rather he has a very real stake in the successful outcome of the experiment.

—Martin T. Orne[1]

Why Study the Volunteer Subject?

We have examined the nature of artifacts attributable to the intentional or unintentional behavior of the researcher and to the participants' sensitivity to particular demand cues. Some participants, those who volunteer for participation in research, seem particularly sensitive and accommodating to demand cues. But even if we did not have to concern ourselves with the potential biasing effects of experimenters' expectations or participants' responsiveness to demand characteristics, another question concerns the generalizability of the research results. There is a long-standing fear among researchers that those individuals who find their way into the role of "research subject" may not be representative of the population in general. Insofar as this is true, the generalizability of the results is in jeopardy.

For example, Henry K. Beecher speculated on how volunteers for medical experiments might be motivated by goals that would differentiate them from the rest of population in other basic ways.[2] They might volunteer to obtain free medical care, to relieve their boredom, or to benefit financially. If it were wartime and they were conscientious objectors, they might volunteer to avoid their military obligation or to contribute to the maintenance of the national health. If they were pacifists or members of religious groups, they might want to participate in research to receive some spiritual reward. And, as Orne was quoted in the previous chapter as saying, people volunteer in the hope of helping science.[3] Whatever the particular motive for volunteering, it is conceivable that the person's special status as a volunteer participant may impose limitations on the generalizability of the research results.

In particular, to the extent that people who volunteer are different from nonvolunteers, the use of volunteer participants may seriously affect the estimates of such parameters as means, medians, proportions, variances, skewness, and kurtosis. In survey research, where the estimation of such parameters for one or more samples is the main goal, any biasing effects of volunteer participants could be disastrous. This problem had been of concern to statisticians and social scientists long before it attracted our attention. They devoted considerable effort to documenting the effects of *nonresponse bias* (error due to nonresponse or nonparticipation) on the accuracy of estimates of various population values,[4] and we will show how volunteer bias (systematic error due to the participants' volunteer status) was operationally defined in this research.

In a good deal of behavioral research, interest is centered more on such statistics as the differences between means and proportions. The experimental investigator is ordinarily interested in relating such differences to the operation of an independent variable. That volunteers differ from nonvolunteers in their scores on the dependent variable may be of little interest to the behavioral experimenter, who wants only to know whether the magnitude of the differences between the experimental and control group means would be affected if the participants were volunteers. In other words, the experimenter is interested in discovering whether the participants' volunteer status interacts with the experimental variable. In due course, we shall see that such interactions do indeed occur. Orne's research provided a hint when he spoke of using only *volunteer* participants in his studies of the good subject effect.

Another reason for studying the volunteer has developed out of federal and professional directives that call for the use of informed participants.[5] Bureaucracies, formalities, and legalities that did not exist a generation or more ago have made the requirements for research with human participants increasingly demanding. A possible outcome is that the behavioral science of the future will be based only on the responses of volunteers who have been made fully aware of the variables of interest to the investigator. Even without this extreme consequence, it is important to understand the circumstances determining what makes one person volunteer and what inhibits another from doing so.

Quantifying Volunteer Bias

As noted, *volunteer bias* refers to the systematic error resulting when participants who volunteer respond differently from how people in the general population would respond. Table 5.1 provides some relevant data presented by William G. Cochran, a statistician, in his discussion of nonresponse bias.[6] Three waves of questionnaires were mailed out to fruit growers, and the number of growers responding to each of the three waves was recorded, as was the number of growers who never responded.

Table 5.1

Example of Volunteer Bias in Survey Research

	First wave	Second wave	Third wave	Total non-respondents	Total population
			Response to three mailings		
Basic data					
1. Number of respondents	300	543	434	1839	3116
2. Proportion of population	.10	.17	.14	.59	1.00
3. Mean trees per respondent	456	382	340	290	329
Cumulative data					
4. Mean trees per respondent (Y_1)	456	408	385	–	–
5. Mean trees per nonrespondent (Y_2)	315	300	290	–	–
6. Difference ($Y_1 - Y_2$)	141	108	95	–	–
7. Proportion of nonrespondents (P)	.90	.73	.59	–	–
8. Bias $P(Y_1 - Y_2)$	127	79	56	–	–

One question dealt with the number of fruit trees owned; for just this question, data were available for the entire population of growers. Because of this fortunate circumstance, we can estimate the degree of volunteer bias present after the first, second, and third waves of questionnaires. The table shows these calculations and gives the formal statistical definition provided for volunteer bias.

The first three rows in this table give all the basic data: (1) the number of respondents (volunteers) and nonrespondents (nonvolunteers) to each wave of questionnaires; (2) the proportion of the total population represented by each wave of respondents and nonrespondents; and (3) the mean number of trees actually owned by each wave of respondents and nonrespondents. Examination of the third row reveals the nature of the volunteer bias: the earlier responders owned more trees, on average, than did the later responders. The remaining rows of data are based on the cumulative number of respondents available after the first, second, and third waves. For each of these waves, five items of information are provided: (4) the mean number of trees owned by the respondents up to that point in the survey (Y_1); (5) the mean number of trees of those who had not yet responded (Y_2); (6) the difference between these two values ($Y_1 - Y_2$); (7) the proportion of the population that had not yet responded (P); and (8) the magnitude of the bias, defined as $P(Y_1 - Y_2)$.

An examination of row 8 shows that, with each successive wave of respondents, there was an appreciable decrease in the magnitude of the volunteer bias. This is a fairly typical result, that increasing the effort to recruit the nonvolunteer decreases the bias in the sample estimates. Of concern to us, however, is that, in most circumstances of behavioral research, we can compute only the proportion of our population who failed to participate (P) and the statistic of interest for those who volunteered or responded (Y_1). That is, we cannot usually compute the statistic of interest for those who did not volunteer or respond (Y_2). It is our lot usually to be in a position to suspect bias, but to be unable to give an accurate quantitative statement about its magnitude. However, as we will show later, we can often speculate on the direction of that bias and use this information to help us interpret the results.

Reliability of Volunteering

Before going any further in this discussion, it is important to examine the assumption that volunteering for research is a reliable event. If it were a purely random event, we could not expect to find any stable relationships between volunteering and various personal characteristics. As we will see, a good many other characteristics have been found to relate predictably to volunteering. The reliability of the act of volunteering, then, cannot reasonably be expected to be zero on psychometric grounds alone. Table 5.2 gives us further reasons to believe that volunteering for research participation is a reliable event. The table summarizes the results of a set of studies in which the reliabilities were reported, or in which there were sufficient raw ingredients for us to estimate the reliabilities ourselves.

For the 10 studies shown, the median reliability coefficient is .52, with a range from .22 to .97. As a standard against which to compare these values, we chose the subtest intercorrelations for what is perhaps the most widely used and carefully developed test of intelligence, the Wechsler Adult Intelligence Scale (WAIS).[7] Repeated factor analyses of this test have shown that there is a very large first factor (often referred to as g), that typically accounts for 10 times more variance than other factors extracted. Subtest intercorrelations for the WAIS were reported by David Wechsler to range from .08 to .85, with a median of .52; this median is, by coincidence, the median value of the reliabilities of volunteering for research shown in Table 5.2.

Eight of the studies in this table requested volunteering for laboratory research, while two studies requested cooperation in survey research conducted in the field. The median reliability of the laboratory studies was .56, while the median for the field studies was .41. Five studies requested people to volunteer or respond a second time for the same task. In the remaining five studies, the second and later requests were for volunteering for a

Table 5.2

The Reliability of Volunteering Behavior

Type of study	Correlation	p
Choice-reaction[a]	.22	.05
Interviews[b]	.24	.02
Personality[c]	.34	.05
Various experiments[d]	.42	.001
Various experiments[d]	.45	.001
Questionnaires[e]	.58	.001
Sex[f]	.67	.001
Personality[f]	.80	.001
Learning[f]	.91	.001
Hypnosis[f]	.97	.001
Median	.52	.001

[a]D. R. J. Laming, "On Procuring Human Subjects," *Quarterly Journal of Experimental Psychology,* 1967, vol. 19, pp. 64–69. All of the subjects had been volunteers at one time, so that the reliability was probably lowered by a restriction of range of the volunteering variable.

[b]B. S. Dohrenwend and B. P. Dohrenwend, "Sources of Refusals in Surveys," *Public Opinion Quarterly,* 1968, vol. 32, pp. 74–83. All of the subjects had been volunteers at one time, so that the reliability was probably lowered by a restriction of range of the volunteering variable. In this study, the second request was to volunteer for the same research as the first request.

[c]E. Rosen, "Differences Between Volunteers and Non-volunteers for Psychological Studies," *Journal of Applied Psychology,* 1951, vol. 35, pp. 185–193.

[d]J. C. Barefoot, "Anxiety and Volunteering," *Psychonomic Science,* 1969, vol. 16, pp. 283–284.

[e]D. Wallace, "A Case For-and-Against Mail Questionnaires," *Public Opinion Quarterly,* 1954, vol. 18, pp. 40–52.

[f]R. M. Martin and F. L. Marcuse, "Characteristics of Volunteers and Nonvolunteers in Psychological Experimentation," *Journal of Consulting Psychology,* 1958, vol. 22, pp. 475–479. In all these studies, the second request was to volunteer for the same research as the first request.

different study. If there were propensities to volunteer, then these propensities should be more stable when persons were asked to volunteer for the same, rather than a different, type of research experience. The median reliability for studies requesting volunteers for the same task was .80, while the median reliability for studies requesting volunteers for different tasks was .42.

Although 10 studies is not very many, the results of these studies raise the possibility that volunteering has general and specific predictors. Presumably, some people volunteer reliably more than others for a variety of tasks, and these reliable individual differences may become further stabilized in a specific consideration of the particular task for which volunteering was requested.

Comparing Volunteers and Nonvolunteers

You may be asking yourself how one goes about comparing the volunteers and nonvolunteers, because the nonvolunteers are, by definition, those people who choose not to participate. Several procedures have been found useful, and they can be grouped into one of two types: the exhaustive and the nonexhaustive.[8] In the exhaustive approach, all the prospective participants are identified by their status on all the variables on which the volunteers and nonvolunteers are to be compared. If the setting is academic, all the students who are prospective participants might be tested first on some required measure and their biographical information would be collected. For example, incoming freshmen are routinely administered a battery of tests in many colleges. At some later point, the students would be recruited for research participation, and the demographic and test data of those who volunteered would be compared with the measurements of those who turned down the request.

A variation on this approach is to recruit participants in a college class. The names of the volunteers and nonvolunteers are sorted from the roster of all students. Shortly after, a test or some other material is administered to the entire class by someone unrelated to the person who recruited the volunteers. How the volunteers and nonvolunteers did on the test or other material is then extracted from these data. In all cases, the assumption made is that the anonymity of the volunteers and the nonvolunteers will be protected by the use of a code, so that only the fact that a person did or did not volunteer is contained in the research record.

In the nonexhaustive approach, data are not available for all of the potential participants, but data are available for those differing in the likelihood of finding their way into a final sample. One variation uses the easy-to-recruit person. We tap a population of volunteer participants repeatedly so as to compare second-stage volunteers with first-stage volunteers, and so on. Suppose the repeated volunteers were higher in the need for social approval than the one-time volunteers. By extrapolating from these data roughly to the zero level of volunteering, we can conclude that nonvolunteers may be lower still in approval need.

Another variation on the nonexhaustive approach gets at the hard-to-recruit individuals. The incentive to participate is repeatedly increased (within ethically approved limits), as in survey research that tries to coax more respondents into the sampling pool by increasing the incentive. We can also focus on the slow-to-reply person. In this case, only a single request for volunteers is issued, and the latency of volunteering is the criterion for dividing up the waves of respondents as well as the basis for extrapolating to the nonrespondents.

Characteristics of the Volunteer Subject

With these and other approaches to identifying volunteers and nonvolunteers, hundreds of results have been gathered. Based on an analysis of such results some years ago, we identified 17 characteristics that distinguished volunteers from nonvolunteers,[9] summarized as main effects in Table 5.3. The rows indicate each characteristic, and the first column of data shows the number of studies providing evidence on the relationship

Table 5.3

Summary of Studies of Volunteer Characteristics

Characteristics of the volunteer subject	Numbers of studies	Percentage of total studies significantly favoring the conclusion	Percentage of significant studies favoring the conclusion
"Maximum" confidence			
1. Better educated	26	92	100
2. Higher social class	46	70	86
3. Intelligent	37	54	91
4. Approval-motivated	19	58	100
5. Sociable	19	63	92
"Considerable" confidence			
6. Arousal-seeking	26	50	81
7. Unconventional	20	55	73
8. Female	63	35	79
9. Nonauthoritarian	34	35	80
10. Jewish or Protestant	17	41	100
11. Nonconforming	17	29	100
"Some" confidence			
12. From smaller towns	10	40	100
13. Interested in religion	11	36	80
14. Altruistic	4	100	100
15. Self-disclosing	3	100	100
16. Maladjusted	34	44	62
17. Young	41	34	61

between volunteering and the characteristic in question. The minimum requirement for admission to this list was at least three statistically significant results, in either direction, bearing on the relationship between any characteristic and volunteering. The total studies found to be significant (not in this table) ranged from 29% ("Nonconforming") to 100% ("Self-disclosing" and "Altruistic").

The next column in Table 5.3 shows the percentage of the total number of relevant results that reported a statistically significant relationship between volunteering and the named characteristic of volunteers. For example, row 8 shows that there were 63 studies of the relationship between gender and research volunteering, and that 35% of these studies found that females were more likely than males to volunteer for research participation. This finding does not rule out the possibility that an equally large percentage of the total number of relevant studies had yielded results statistically significant in the opposite direction. To control for this possibility, the next column shows the net evidence for each specific relationship, that is, the percentage of all statistically significant results that favored the particular conclusion reached.

Also indicated in Table 5.3 is a "confidence level" we can recommend based on this analysis. It is not a confidence level in the statistical sense but reflects the inductive confidence we have in a conclusion based on the number of studies and the direction of the majority of results. To qualify for "maximum confidence," a characteristic had to be based on a large number of studies (at least 19), of which a majority significantly favored the conclusion, and of which the vast majority (86%) of just the significant outcomes also favored the conclusion drawn. To qualify for "considerable confidence," a large number of studies was also required (at least 17), but the fraction of total studies "significantly" in support of the characteristic was permitted to drop somewhat below one third; the percentage of significant results that favored the conclusion was still required to be large (73%). The major difference between the categories of "considerable" and "some" confidence was in the number of studies available on which to base a conclusion (at least 3 in the case of "some confidence"); the fraction of total studies "significantly" supporting a characteristic remained at about one third (34%), but the percentage of significant results favoring the conclusion was still relatively substantial (61%).

To view this subjective grouping in a slightly different way, we can say that the degree of confidence in a characteristic was based on the extent to which future studies reporting no statistically significant relationship, or even relationships significantly in the opposite direction, would be unlikely to alter the overall conclusion drawn. For example, if 24 of 26 studies showed volunteers to be significantly better educated than nonvolunteers, it would take a great many studies showing no significant relationship, and even a fair number of studies showing a significantly opposite relationship, for us to decide that volunteers were not, on the whole, better educated than nonvolunteers. This analysis is nevertheless a crude procedure, but we understand that meta-analytic work is currently under way to evaluate all the findings to date. Such an analysis will give us a sharper picture of the typical magnitude of differences between volunteers and nonvolunteers, but for the time being, we can rely on this analysis.

One limitation of the summary of characteristics in Table 5.3 is that they tell us nothing about racial or ethnic differences in volunteering; these variables await further study. The summary is also limited by the fact that the variables noted are not qualified by the particular task for which volunteering was requested. That is, this summary is robust in the sense that conclusions drawn with good levels of confidence transcend the effects of possible moderator variables. However, the conclusions are not as precise as they might have been had they taken into account the effects of possible moderator variables. Fortunately, such information is available, although the stated conclusions become somewhat more cumbersome when we increase the precision of specification. We will go through the list in Table 5.3 and this time flesh out the conclusions. Where there appear to be inconsistencies, it is useful to keep in mind that the operationalization of some variables is based on specific psychological instruments (e.g., intelligence refers to IQ test scores, and authoritarianism is also based on test scores) rather than on behavior.

Conclusions Warranting "Maximum" Confidence
(1) Volunteers tend to be better educated than nonvolunteers, especially when personal contact between the researcher and the participant is not required. (2) Volunteers tend to have higher social-class status than nonvolunteers, especially when social class can be defined by the participants' own status rather than by parental status. (3) Volunteers tend to be higher in intelligence than nonvolunteers when recruitment is for research in general, but not when recruitment is for less typical types of research, such as hypnosis, sensory isolation, sexual studies, and small-group and personality research. (4) Volunteers tend to be higher in the need for social approval than nonvolunteers. (5) Volunteers tend to be more sociable than nonvolunteers.

Conclusions Warranting "Considerable" Confidence
(6) Volunteers tend to be more arousal-seeking than nonvolunteers, especially when recruitment is for studies of stress, sensory isolation, and hypnosis. (7) Volunteers tend to be more unconventional than nonvolunteers, particularly if recruitment is for studies of sexual behavior. (8) Females are more likely than males to volunteer for research in general, but females are less likely to volunteer for physically and emotionally stressful research (e.g., electric shock, high temperature, sensory deprivation, and interviews about sexual behavior). (9) Volunteers tend to be less authoritarian than nonvolunteers. (10) Jews are more likely to volunteer than Protestants, and Protestants are more likely to volunteer than Catholics. (11) Volunteers tend to be less conforming than nonvolunteers when recruitment is for research in general, but not when women are recruited for hypnosis, sleep, or counseling research.

Conclusions Warranting "Some" Confidence (12) Volunteers tend to be from smaller towns than nonvolunteers, especially in questionnaire studies. (13) Volunteers tend to be more interested in religion than nonvolunteers, again especially in questionnaire studies. (14) Volunteers tend to be more altruistic than nonvolunteers. (15) Volunteers tend to be more self-disclosing than nonvolunteers. (16) Volunteers tend to be more maladjusted than nonvolunteers, especially when recruitment is for an unusual situation (e.g., drug research, hypnosis, high-temperature research, or vaguely described experiments) or for medical research employing a clinical (rather than a psychometric) definition of psychopathology. (17) Volunteers tend to be younger than nonvolunteers, especially when women are recruited for laboratory research.

Situational Determinants of Volunteering

A similar analysis was possible of the relationship between volunteering and certain situational moderators.[10] As in our discussion of the more stable characteristics of volunteers, our inventory of situational determinants was developed inductively rather than deductively. In this case, we asked what situational variables increased or decreased the rate of volunteering. The answer to this question has implications for both the theory and the practice of the behavioral sciences. If we can learn more about the situational influences on volunteering, we will also have learned more about social influence in general—which is what McGuire (Chapter 1) implied when he spoke about exploiting "artifacts" as variables of interest in their own right. If we learn more about the situational determinants of volunteering, we may also be in a better position to reduce the bias in our samples that derives from volunteers' being systematically different from nonvolunteers in a variety of characteristics.

The results bearing on the relationship between volunteering and situational variables were not as plentiful or as direct as they were in the preceding case. We again list (below) the variables by the degree of confidence we can have that each is actually associated with volunteering. Three groups of determinants were discriminable, and within each group, the determinants could be listed in approximately descending order of the degree of confidence we can have in the relationship between volunteering and the listed determinant. As before, the definition of degree of confidence was based both on the number of studies relevant to the relationship under consideration and on the proportion of relevant studies whose results supported a specific directional conclusion.

To qualify for "maximum confidence," a relationship now had to be based on at least 20 studies, and at least 6 out of 7 studies had to support the specific conclusion. Two conclusions met these criteria: (1) People who are more interested in the topic under investigation are more likely to volunteer, and (2) people with expectations of being favorably evaluated by the investigator are more likely to volunteer.

To qualify for "considerable confidence," a relationship had to be based on at least 10 studies with at least two thirds supporting the conclusion. Three additional conclusions met these criteria: (3) People who perceive the investigation as important are likely to volunteer. (4) People's feeling states at the time of the request for volunteers are likely to affect the probability of volunteering; people who are made to "feel good" or to feel competent are more likely to volunteer. (5) People who are offered greater material incentives are likely to volunteer, especially if the incentives are offered as gifts in advance and without being contingent on the person's decision to volunteer.

To qualify for "some confidence," a relationship had to be based either on 3 studies, all of which were in support of the relationship, or on 9 studies, most of which were in support of the relationship and of which none showed a significant reversal of the relationship. Three final conclusions met these criteria: (6) Personal characteristics of the recruiter are likely to affect the prospective participant's probability of volunteering. Recruiters higher in status or prestige are likely to obtain higher rates of volunteering, as are female recruiters; this latter relationship is especially modifiable by the sex of the prospective participant and the nature of the research. (7) People are less likely to volunteer for tasks that are more aversive in the sense of being painful, stressful, or dangerous biologically or psychologically. Personal characteristics of the prospective participant and the level of the incentive offered may moderate the relationship between volunteering and task aversiveness. (8) People are more likely to volunteer when volunteering is viewed as the normative, expected, appropriate thing to do.

One implication of these eight conclusions is that, at least in theory, we can do something to improve the representativeness of our participant samples. For example, we can make the appeal for volunteering as interesting as possible (keeping in mind the nature of the target population) and make it as nonthreatening as possible so that potential volunteers will not be put off by unwarranted fears of unfavorable evaluation. We can also state the theoretical and practical importance of the research and state in what way the target population is relevant to the research and their social responsibility to participate in research that has the potential of benefiting others. We can, when possible, offer to pay prospective volunteers for participating and offer a small courtesy gift for taking the time to consider whether they will participate. We can have the request for volunteering made by a person of high status, preferably by a woman. We can try to avoid tasks that may be psychologically or biologically stressful. Finally, we can have someone known to the potential participants make the appeal for volunteers. If volunteering is regarded by these potential participants as normative (that is, typical in this population), we might ask for public commitment (a show of hands); if nonvolunteering is normative, we might ask for private commitment.

Volunteer Status and Research Outcomes

In the previous chapter, we described a scaling study of the role expectations of prospective participants. In that study were people who had volunteered for another research study and people who had not volunteered, and thus we were able to compare the scaling responses of these two groups. Some of the items were repeated in the questionnaire, and for each person in the volunteer sample and the nonvolunteer sample, we correlated the responses to the items. The responses made by the volunteers were more reliable (median r = .68) than the responses made by the nonvolunteers (median r = .48). In terms of psychometric implications, the volunteers provided "better data" for the scaling solution. The psychological implication of the difference in the reliabilities was not entirely clear, but we thought that the volunteers, being brighter and higher in the need for social approval, may have *tried* to be more consistent.

In another set of studies, we identified the volunteers and the nonvolunteers by using the exhaustive approach described previously, in which research participants are recruited in a college class: All the students—volunteers and nonvolunteers—participate in another study, and their responses in this second study provide the basic data for a comparison of the two groups. In one such investigation, Rosnow and Jerry M. Suls studied the responses of college students in a standard opinion-change experiment using a persuasive message as the treatment. The Solomon design was used for the purpose of identifying and comparing any effects of pretest sensitization in the volunteers and the non-volunteers.[11] It will be recalled that *pretest sensitization bias* refers to the potential biasing effect of an instrument (e.g., a questionnaire) that precedes the treatment and is again administered after the treatment. The Solomon design calls for four randomly assigned groups: two are pretested, and the other two are not pretested. Within the pretested and nonpretested groups, one group is administered the treatment and the other is not. By comparing the posttest means of these four groups, we can find out the direction and magnitude of any pretest sensitization bias effects that occurred.

It had been theorized that pretesting should heighten the volunteers' responsiveness to demand cues, informing them that some change is expected.[12] Nonvolunteers, on the other hand, may be less responsive or even resistant to such cues. The point is that, besides possibly magnifying or washing out the effects of the treatment, the pretesting of volunteers may produce a different biasing effect than the pretesting of nonvolunteers. The findings in this study showed that the volunteers, in comparison with the nonvolunteers, were overly responsive to the treatment after being pretested. The pretest sensitization responses of the nonvolunteers were in the opposite direction of the volunteers' responses. Another investigation in this series, done with Jeffrey H. Goldstein, Barry E. Goodstadt, and Jerry M. Suls,[13] studied the potential biasing effect of the participants' volunteer status in verbal operant-conditioning research, and once again, the results were that volunteers tended to be overly accommodating to demand cues.

Some researchers had questioned the pervasiveness of such "volunteer artifacts,"[14] but studies like these implied that biasing effects might be quite pervasive. Several hundred studies had previously used the verbal conditioning paradigm with volunteer participants, and a large number of laboratory social influence studies had used the pretest-posttest design without the requisite controls for pretest sensitization. In addition, studies by other investigators implicated volunteer artifacts in a wide variety of situations. For example, I. A. Horowitz reported that volunteers responded differently from nonvolunteers to fear-arousing communications, a result that he argued helped to resolve inconsistencies in the conclusions previously reported by a number of investigators working in this area.[15] H. Kotses, K. D. Glaus, and L. E. Fisher reported the occurrence of volunteer artifacts in an experimental study of physiological responses to random bursts of white noise.[16] R. W. Black, J. Schumpert, and F. A. Welch reported that perceptual-motor responses were confounded by the participants' volunteer status.[17] Volunteer bias has also been implied in clinical and counseling studies.[18]

Power and the Pseudovolunteer

Another useful finding in this area concerned the concept of power in statistical significance testing. *Power* refers to the probability of not overlooking an effect or a relationship that is "really there." As described previously, the effect size is a measure of the magnitude of the relationship between the independent and dependent variables. When we do statistical significance testing, a basic assumption is that the significance test chosen (e.g., the *t* test or the *F* test) must be "powerful" enough to detect an obtained effect at a specified level of significance. In Chapter 3, we noted that the magnitude of a significance test is equivalent to the size of the effect times the size of the study. The size of study was defined as the sample size; if the sample is too small, it is possible that an obtained effect will go undetected at the specified significance level. Given an estimated effect size, we can consult a table to determine how many participants we must recruit.[19]

The problem is that not everyone who is recruited may show up at the scheduled time. If we were counting on a particular number of people to show up, we would have to make an allowance for the no-shows (also called *pseudovolunteers*) by recruiting more people.[20] Our analysis of the literature on no-shows turned up 20 studies, and the results are shown in the stem-and-leaf plot in Table 5.4. Each row label is called a *stem;* these "stem ends" show leading digits from .4 to .0. The leaves are the second digits, which in combination with the leading digits tell us there were .40, .41, and .42 no-shows in three studies denoted in the first row of this stem-and-leaf. The summary data at the bottom of the table indicate that the median proportion of no-shows

Table 5.4

Proportions of No-Shows in 20 Studies

Stems	Leaves								
.4	0	1	2						
.3	0	0	1	2	6	6	7	7	7	8
.2	4								
.1	0	2	4	6	9				
.0	3								

Maximum value	.42
75th percentile	.37
Median	.315
25th percentile	.17
Minimum value	.03

was almost one third (.315). Suppose we were counting on a sample size of 40 participants and wanted to make an allowance for the no-shows. These data suggest that we should schedule about 60 people, on the assumption that one third may not show up.

Predicting the Direction of Bias

Granted that volunteers are never a random sample of the population from which they were recruited, and that any given sample of volunteers may differ from nonvolunteers on a number of dimensions, we can view the threat to generalizability of using volunteer subjects as a specific case of sampling bias. The question of interest is whether the resulting bias will lead us to overestimate or underestimate the population's parameters. We cannot be absolutely certain that, in any given study, the performance of the volunteer participants differed from the potential performance of the unsampled nonvolunteers if they had participated in the study. However, based on what we have learned about the characteristics of volunteers, we can predict the direction of volunteer bias in many situations.

Figure 5.1 helps us illustrate this idea in the specific case of IQ testing. Previously it was concluded that volunteers tend to score higher on intelligence tests than nonvolunteers. If we relied solely on volunteer participants to develop norms for an IQ test, it follows that the estimated population mean would be artificially inflated by this sampling procedure. In this figure, the curve called Y represents a theoretical normal distribution of IQs in the general population; the curve called X represents a theoretical normal distribution of IQs among volunteers. To the extent that the mean of X is different from the mean of Y, the resulting bias constitutes a threat to the generalizability of the data. Merely increasing the size of the sample would not reduce this bias, unless we made an effort to improve the representativeness of the sampling procedures as well. However, at least we are able to predict the direction of the volunteer bias.

Another example of this type of sampling bias was described by A. H. Maslow and J. M. Sakoda, who contended that volunteer bias may have had grave effects on Alfred C. Kinsey's classic estimates of human sexual behavior.[21] Kinsey and his associates had conducted a series of intensive interviews of some 8,000 American men and 12,000 American women in order to uncover the predominant sexual customs in the United States.[22] Their fascinating findings became a source of intense discussion and controversy when the question of sampling bias was raised by critics.[23] Might Kinsey's respondents, by virtue of their willingness to answer his questions, have shared other attributes that distinguished them from the rest of the population and thereby restricted the generalizability of the data?

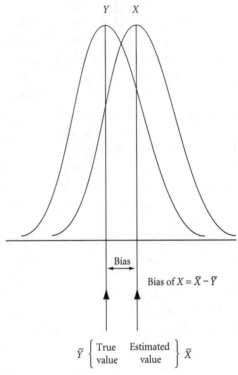

Figure 5.1 The curve symbolized as Y represents a theoretical normal distribution of IQs in the general population, and the curve labeled X represents a theoretical normal distribution of IQs among volunteers. To the extent that the mean of X is different from the mean of Y, the resultant bias constitutes a threat to the generalizability of the data.

Maslow and Sakoda addressed this question in a study they designed with Kinsey. It was arranged for him to set up an office near the Brooklyn College campus and for Maslow to make an appeal for volunteers in his classes. Earlier, Maslow had found that people high in self-esteem reported having relatively unconventional sexual attitudes and behavior,[24] and he and Sakoda now found that students who volunteered for a Kinsey interview scored higher in self-esteem than nonvolunteers for an interview. Putting these findings together, Maslow and Sakoda concluded that Kinsey's sample estimates had exaggerated the true population values.[25]

We can conceive of many nonexperimental situations in which we should be able to predict the direction of volunteer bias. For example, given that volunteers are less authoritarian than nonvolunteers (Characteristic 9 in Table 5.3), were we to employ volunteers to provide the norms for a test that correlated positively with authoritarianism, we would anticipate underestimating the population mean. The point is that, insofar as any of the characteristics listed previously can be conceptualized as a potential threat to generalizability, we can predict the direction of this threat.

In survey research, where the estimation of one or more parameters is the goal, the biasing effects of volunteer samples could be disastrous. In most behavioral experiments, however, interest is not centered so much on means and proportions as on the differences between means or proportions. Experimenters are interested in relating such differences to the operation of their independent variables. That volunteers may differ from nonvolunteers in scores on the dependent variable may be irrelevant to the behavioral experimenter, who is more interested in the magnitude and statistical significance level of the difference between the experimental and the control group means. In this case as well, however, we can predict whether the participants' volunteer status may have combined with the experimental variable.

Suppose we wanted to test the effects of some experimental manipulation on the dependent variable of gregariousness. If we drew a sample of volunteers, any treatment designed to increase gregariousness might be too harshly judged as ineffective because the untreated control group would already be unusually high on the factor of sociability (Characteristic 5 in Table 5.3). The same treatment might prove effective in increasing the gregariousness of the experimental group relative to the control group if the total sample were characterized by a less restricted range of sociability. Another example of this direction of bias would be if we wanted to assess the validity of a new educational procedure that was purported to make people less rigid in their thinking. If we randomly assigned volunteers to an experimental group that received the procedure or to a control group that did not receive it, we would predict that the controls would already be unusually low on the dependent variable (because volunteers are low in authoritarianism). Thus we would again have minimized the true difference between the two groups by using just volunteer participants.

The opposite type of error can also be imagined. Suppose we wanted to find out how persuasive a propaganda appeal was by using a sample of volunteers, half of whom would receive the message (the experimental group) and half of whom would not (the control group). Given that volunteers tend to be higher in the need for social approval (Characteristic 4 in Table 5.3), and that people who are high in the need for social approval are more readily influenced than people low in this need, we would predict that participants exposed to the experimental treatment would overreact to it. Comparing their pre-to-post scores with those in the control group would exaggerate the true impact of the propaganda.

Previously we mentioned that one reason for our interest in the volunteer subject has to do with the proliferation of ethical directives and the possibility that we may often find ourselves able to work only with volunteers. Because of ethical rules that insist on the use of informed participants, the behavioral science of the future may be based not on McNemar's "college sopho-mores," but on *volunteer* sophomores who have been made fully aware of the responses of interest to the researcher. As we will see next, ethical limitations imposed by statutory, institutional, and professional directives present a challenge to researchers to build a methodologically stronger, as well as more ethical, science.

Chapter 6

Ethical and Methodological Challenges

We might say that science is a calling and not an occupation only, or at any rate, that it cannot flourish if it is always an occupation only. And the difference between these two sorts of pursuits lies in this, that we choose an occupation while a calling chooses us; we are impelled to the calling from within, which is to say that we are committed to its values.

—Abraham Kaplan[1]

Tides of Change

One consequence of the artifact assault of the 1960s and 1970s was to call attention to limitations of experimental methods in behavioral science. Yet it was by experimentation that researchers had demonstrated the existence of artifacts. (The irony of this situation did not escape the critics of the artifact work or the artifactologists themselves, neither of whom wished to abandon the method of experimentation.) This work had made the artifactologists superconscious of both the utility and the limits of behavioral experimentation. It also underscored the fact that the ship of behavioral science is never finished and, as in all areas of science, is in a constant state of reconstruction. The problem was not simply that the method of experimentation was imperfect, because the same criticism could be leveled against any method of inquiry. The problem was to identify particular limitations and then to use multiple methods of inquiry, each imperfect in some way, to triangulate on the question or hypothesis of scientific interest.[2]

In the 1960s and 1970s, we also learned that every method of inquiry, as well as the basic facts acquired through the use of each method, could be understood only in a particular context of explanation and that methods that had seemed quite appropriate at one time were now seen as ethically problematic in some way.[3] For example, if we think back to the heyday of experimental social psychology in the 1950s and 1960s, we are reminded that many of the seminal studies that were conducted then would be impossible today (e.g., Milgram's obedience studies). The reason for this change is that daunting arrays of ethical issues had not been raised a generation or more ago in the form that they have today.[4] New researchers who practice their calling in the years ahead will need to anticipate such issues and to take a constructive, problem-solving approach when faced with ethical problems.

In this final chapter, we will sketch what we perceive as a constantly changing montage of ethical issues. We will touch on the events leading up to the present situation and examine the moral dilemma faced by new researchers, who may find themselves caught between the Scylla of methodological requirements and the Charybdis of ethical demands. Picking up a thread from some previous work,[5] we will describe how a confrontation between the technical and the moral provides opportunities to strengthen our science: we can strive to develop scientific and analytic insights that will enhance the ethical nature of our research *and* its technical merit.

Ethics and Artifacts in Collision

The term *ethics,* as used here, refers to the moral standards or values by which human conduct is judged. Applied to research in the behavioral sciences, ethical guidelines allow us to judge the morality of scientific conduct no matter who the researcher is, as long as the research situation is similar. In psychology, for example, such guidelines enable researchers to anticipate suspected transgressions and to decide how to avoid or rectify ethical problems. Stretching our imagination, we can envision these collective guidelines as an idealized "social contract" of do's and don'ts. Each new generation of researchers is required to subscribe to some form of such a contract as a moral prerequisite of conducting research with human participants. Broadly speaking, the moral agreement in behavioral research can be described as the responsibility *not to do* physical or psychological harm to the participants and *to do* beneficent research in a way that is likely to produce valid results.

For example, as part of their research training, doctoral students in psychology are instructed about the ethical ideal known as *informed consent,* which is one "contractual" obligation in human participant research. The principle of informed consent was predicated on the assumption that participants are entitled to know what they were getting into; informed consent guidelines tell us to acquaint potential participants with the essential facts of a study (such as its purpose and the nature of the instruments used). One source of concern in some areas is that, as a result of statutory requirements, it has become necessary to add further details to the informed consent form (i.e., the document that the participant signs to indicate his or her understanding of the nature of the study and willingness to take part). As well meaning as these requirements are, they often result in forms that are both cumbersome and hard to understand. One researcher reported that people believed they had relinquished their right to sue for negligence by signing the form, although that right is legally protected.[6]

However, a perennial question has been whether compliance with human participant regulations presents a dilemma for researchers who are also concerned about avoiding or minimizing artifacts.[7] An early study by Jerome H. Resnick and Thomas Schwartz implied that there was a delicate balance between ethics and participant-related artifacts.[8] The investigators used a traditional verbal conditioning procedure, the Taffel task,[9] in an experiment in which they manipulated the ethical standard of informed consent. The participants received a sequence of cards, one card at a time, each of which showed a specific verb and the six pronouns *I, you, we, he, she,* and *they;* the instructions were to use the verb shown on the card to compose a sentence beginning with one of the pronouns. The experimenter responded, "Good" or "OK" each time the participant selected *I* or *we,* the object being to condition the participant to choose only these two pronouns. Half of the potential participants were explicitly informed of the nature of the conditioning procedure in strict adherence with proposed informed-consent guidelines; the other potential participants were not given this information, and the experiment was run in the way it would have been before the era of informed consent.

One finding was that not only was it more difficult to get the ethically informed people to agree to participate in the study, but more than half of the ethically informed volunteers were no-shows, whereas all the "uninformed" volunteers appeared at the appointed time and place. The result of major interest, however, was that the uninformed group was conditioned as expected, but the informed group responded in the opposite direction of conditioning theory. Using postexperimental questionnaires, Resnick and Schwartz discovered that many informed participants, after having been told so much about the study, had carried on a train of thought in which they had questioned the experimenter's "true" hypothesis. One person who had been negatively conditioned stated that he "had wanted to play it cool; and to give the impression that the experimenter's reinforcements were having no effect."[10] When told that his use of the two reinforced pronouns had decreased by more than half from the first 20 trials to the last 20, this person laughed and said, "I was afraid I would overdo it."[11]

It was disturbing to Resnick and Schwartz that ethically informed participants had become distrustful or recalcitrant. Resnick and Schwartz also questioned what was really happening in "a room full of mirrors where objective reality and its perception blend, and thereby become metaphysical."[12] Their results implied that the standard textbook principles of verbal learning might have been reversed if all of the previous studies had strictly adhered to informed-consent rules. More broadly, the results implied that compliance with ethical guidelines presented a dilemma for behavioral researchers who were concerned about minimizing participant-related artifacts. It seemed that compliance with some guidelines was an impediment to the pursuit of knowledge.

Another study implying a potential conflict between ethics and artifacts was reported by Gerald T. Gardner, who had done a series of experiments to explore the effects of noise on task performance.[13] Gardner wanted to replicate a widely cited phenomenon first reported by David Glass and Jerome Singer, indicating that exposure to uncontrollable, unpredictable noise has negative effects on task performance.[14] Although Gardner's initial experiments replicated Glass and Singer's findings, two subsequent studies by Gardner did not, and puzzled by this outcome, he searched for an explanation. The initial studies, like those of Glass and Singer, had been performed before the implementation of federal guidelines requiring informed consent; Gardner's later studies used informed consent.

To assess whether the use of informed consent might have been responsible for the different results, Gardner performed another experiment in which two groups were exposed to uncontrollable noise. Informed consent was used in one group but not in the other. The results of this study implied that the informed-consent procedure had stifled the emergence of negative effects because it had created a perception in the participants of control over the noise. In Gardner's words, perceived control "could result from references . . . in the consent form to subjects' ability to withdraw from the experiment without penalty, to their freedom to choose an alternative to [subject] pool participation."[15] Once again, it appeared that some ethical requirements had put obstacles in the path of progress in behavioral science.

The "Ten Commandments" of the APA

How did the behavioral sciences get into this fix, in which researchers are forced to wrestle with conflicting demands? The roots of this dilemma in psychology go back to the 1960s, when the American public had been whipped into a frenzy of anxiety by reports of domestic wiretapping and other clandestine activities by agencies of the federal government. Caught up in the temper of the times, eminent psychologists began to voice their concerns about the status of human values in their science.[16] For example, Sidney M. Jourard called for a more humanistic research methodology and made explicit references to what he perceived as serious deficiencies in how the experimenter-participant relationship had been defined in psychology.[17] In a similar vein, Herbert Kelman, a leading social psychologist, expressed his disillusionment over what he viewed as the widespread and unquestioned exploitation of "powerless subjects" with abusive deceptions.[18] In Kelman's words,

> What concerns me most is not so much that deception is used, but precisely that it is used without question. . . . I sometimes feel that we are training a generation of students who do not know that there is any other way of doing experiments in our field, who feel that deception

is as much *de rigeur* as significance at the .05 level. Too often deception is used not as a last resort, but as a matter of course. Our attitude seems to be that if you can deceive, why tell the truth?[19]

It did, in fact, seem true that, over the years, both the use and the level of deception had increased. In his early study of conformity in the 1950s, S. E. Asch had had pseudosubjects deceive the participants by keeping a straight face while making ridiculous perceptual judgments about the length of lines.[20] A decade later, Milgram's deception of participants (about applying electric shocks to a "learner" to get him to respond in a particular way) had become a lightning rod for ethical concerns.[21] One survey of research practices in social psychology in the mid-1960s reported that 81 percent of conformity studies and 72 percent of studies on cognitive dissonance and balance theory had routinely used some form of deception.[22] Another report stated that nearly half of the studies published in 1971 in the *Journal of Personality and Social Psychology* had used deception.[23]

The practice of deceiving participants raised methodological red flags as well as ethical concerns. Roger Brown cautioned, "The trouble with deception, morality aside, which it usually is, is that one cannot be sure who is being deceived."[24] Research revealed that some participants became more guarded in their responses once they learned they had been deceived.[25] Still, the use of deception in psychology seemed tame compared to more shocking events elsewhere. In biomedical research, cases of flagrant abuse had come to light, sometimes resulting in the death of human participants.[26] In sociology, where researchers preferred to work in field settings, a graduate student working on his Ph.D. had played the role of homosexual voyeur in order to observe hundreds of homosexual encounters in a public washroom in a city park.[27] In the mid-1960s, when this study was done, sociologists had no code of ethics concerning either the need for informed consent or the inviolability of the right to privacy. Amid unrelenting demands for reform, the question of scientific misconduct became a public issue, discussed in newspapers, magazines, and congressional hearings.[28]

A few years later, privacy as a moral and legal issue had begun to be recognized quite formally, and many Americans were expressing concerns about threats to their "right to be left alone." Behavioral and social scientists who had turned to field research to avoid certain artifacts were no less concerned about the moral or legal issues than those who had turned to laboratory deceptions. Some began to speak about an imbalance between the potential scientific benefits of research and the costs to the rights and welfare of the volunteers who participated in it. John M. Darley argued that there was an ethical imperative in doing sound research because, otherwise, "we leave those who are attempting social change the prey of hucksters who are willing to put forth undocumentable claims based on inadequate evidence."[29] Darley added, however, that researchers had to realize also that "subjects have certain substantive rights that cannot be violated regardless of cost-benefit considerations."[30]

For some time, the American Psychological Association (APA) had, in its code of professional ethics, addressed issues such as the confidentiality of research data. There was now a call for further codification of ethical practices in psychological research. M. Brewster Smith argued that psychological science had become "big business" because of financial support from the federal government, and that researchers were therefore answerable to the public regarding the methods used in studying people.[31] Spurred on by articulate spokespersons, the APA in 1966 created an ad hoc committee—informally called the Cook Commission after Stuart W. Cook, its chair—which was assigned the task of developing a code of ethics for research with human participants. Out of those deliberations came a 1971 draft report,[32] which prompted Resnick and Schwartz to conduct the study mentioned previously. A revised report appeared in 1972, expounding a set of principles[33] that became popularly known as the ten commandments of the American Psychological Association. The complete guidelines were formally adopted by the APA in 1972, were reissued a decade later,[34] and are in the process of being updated by a joint task force of the APA and the American Psychological Society.

The APA's code of research ethics was formulated with the object of informing psychological investigators of their moral responsibilities, helping them decide what aspects of a proposed study might pose an ethical problem, and describing strategies for addressing such problems. For example, the code did not prohibit deception in all research studies but implied *when* a deception might be permissible and noted the attendant ethical responsibilities of the researchers who used deception. By the time of the first adoption of the APA research code, a wide variety of deceptions had slipped into psychological researchers' methodological arsenals.[35] Active deceptions included misrepresenting the purpose of the research or the identity of the researchers, falsely promising something to the participants, misrepresenting the equipment or procedures, and using placebos, pseudosubjects, and secret treatments. Passive deceptions included disguising experiments in natural settings, observing people in a public setting without telling them they were being studied, secretly recording negative behavior, and using projective tests and other measurement techniques without disclosing their purpose to the participants.

Opportunity Knocks More Than Once

The APA code insisted that the use of deception had to be fully justified and that plausible alternatives had to be ruled out; it also required researchers to debrief the participants once the study was over. Debriefing is a good example of how an opportunity to improve the moral condition can be seized on to benefit the pursuit of science. The postexperimental debriefing serves as a kind of "catharsis" to remove misconceptions and anxieties that the participants may have had about the research and to leave them with a sense of dignity and knowledge and a perception of time not wasted.[36] It is also an opportunity to remove any misconceptions of those who were not accepted for participation, for whatever reasons, and were left, as one psychologist put it, "to ponder the significance of their rejection and the implications of the issues raised."[37] In another variation on what Orne called quasi controls, the debriefing session also provides an opportunity to probe what each of the participants thought about the research situation, so that the researcher can develop a phenomenological context in which to interpret the results.[38] This use of the debriefing period has been essential in verifying the efficacy of clinical trials in biomedical studies.[39] The pursuit of scientific knowledge is served because such information can improve the researcher's understanding and interpretation of the research findings and may even provide promising leads for future research.

Some other ideas for fostering a view of research ethics not as an affront to the integrity of sound research, but as giving researchers opportunities for scientific rewards, were recently discussed by Peter Blanck and his coauthors.[40] One ethical principle, which appears in research codes in psychology both in the United States and abroad, is keeping the participants' disclosures confidential.[41] The professional justification for confidentiality in research proceeds on two premises: (1) that we have a professional right to keep our respondents' disclosures private and (2) that we have an ethical obligation to respect their privacy.[42] The potential scientific benefit is that protecting the confidentiality of our participants' responses may also pay off in their responding more openly and honestly.

For example, in one study, the participants were asked to complete a self-report personality measure and a social desirability scale. Some of the participants were promised confidentiality, and the others were not.[43] The results were that the self-report responses were virtually uncorrelated with social desirability in the confidentiality condition but were highly correlated with social desirability in the nonconfidentiality condition. One plausible implication seemed to be that people are more likely to report sensitive information when they know their disclosures will be kept confidential. In a related finding, S. J. Ceci and D. Peters observed that letters of recommendation written by faculty advisers were more critical (i.e., presumably more forthcoming) when the form indicated that the student had waived the right to inspect the letter.[44] This area requires a more detailed analysis to reveal when confidentiality is likely to pay off with more honest responding (and also the legal aspects of confidentiality in research).[45] But the essential point is that respect for confidentiality is a way of encouraging good ethical practices that may provide opportunities for scientific gains as well.

Before moving on, we would like to mention again something that was discussed in the previous chapter. We described some recruitment strategies designed to coax more nonvolunteers into the sampling pool. One recommendation was to tell the potential participants about the true benefits of the research, an approach that has been shown to encourage people to participate. This strategy makes the ethical nature of our work more sound because we are treating our participants as another "granting agency"—which, in fact, they are, granting us precious time, attention, and cooperation. Another side to this strategy is that we are morally obligated not to exaggerate the benefits in order to lure additional people into a research study on false pretenses. We must not tell them that our research is likely to achieve goals that it is unlikely to achieve. An ethical orientation will make us more careful and thoughtful not only in recruiting participants, but in ensuring that our research will be substantive and not trivial.

Not a Cannon, but a Popgun

In the early 1970s, when the Cook Commission produced its draft report,[46] not all psychologists agreed on the necessity for a stringent professional code of research standards. For example, Resnick and Schwartz called for "more understanding of its ramifications concerning the nature of the knowledge it permits us" and advised caution rather than pronouncements.[47] Similarly, Kenneth J. Gergen conceded that there were isolated problems but warned of a possibly dangerous trade-off of scientific advances for excessive ethical constraints:

> Most of us have encountered studies that arouse moral indignation. We do not wish to see such research carried out in the profession. However, the important question is whether the principles we establish to prevent these few experiments from being conducted may not obviate the vast majority of contemporary research. We may be mounting a very dangerous cannon to shoot a mouse.[48]

Interestingly, a survey of a random sample of psychologists and a nonrandom sample of undergraduate students enrolled in an introductory psychology course was conducted around this time to show whether there was a disparity between the ethical viewpoints of psychologists and their typical research participants.[49] Each respondent in the survey was given a hypothetical research case with some controversial design characteristic, such as an experiment that produced stress or pain or altered the participants' self-esteem. The psychologists expressed views of these studies that were much more ethically stringent than those expressed by the students. In fact, in Milgram's obedience work, it seemed that the participants were more tolerant and accepting of even extreme manipulations than most psychologists had imagined. In debriefing his participants, Milgram noted that only 1.3% of them expressed negative feelings about their experimental experience.[50] In any case, the APA's "dangerous cannon" had begun to seem more like a "popgun," particularly in view of the lack of enforcement tools.

Beneficence, Respect, and Justice

To begin to get a sense of where we might be heading in the evolution of ethical imperatives, we can go back to 1973 and the Senate Health Subcommittee hearings chaired by Senator Edward Kennedy. The purpose of the hearings was to investigate abuses in human participant research. Among the prominent cases investigated was a Public Health Service study of untreated syphilis in more than 400 low-income African American men in Tuskegee, Alabama, from 1932 to 1972. The men had been given free health care, including a free annual medical examination, to participate in the study. However, they had been told they would be dropped from the study and lose their care if they sought treatment from any other source. Astoundingly, they had not been told they had syphilis, and when a cure (penicillin) was discovered in 1943, it had not been made available to them. Over the 40 years of this study, the participants had experienced predictable damage to their skeletal, cardiovascular, and central nervous systems and, in some cases, death. After these details were made public by a reporter in 1972, the study was terminated.

In 1974, the National Research Act was passed, requiring the establishment of Institutional Review Boards (IRBs) and creating the National Commission for the Protection of Human Subjects in Biomedical and Behavioral Research.[51] The following year, a directive issued by the U.S. Department of Health, Education, and Welfare (DHEW; now the Department of Health and Human Services, DHHS) ordered that every institution applying for grant support establish a review board to evaluate all grant submissions. If a study were classified by the review board as "at risk," then specific safeguards had to be instituted by the investigators. Such safeguards included giving the research participants an adequate explanation of the procedures to be used, informing them of the potential risks and discomforts, allowing them to ask the researcher any questions they wished, and making sure they understood their prerogative to withdraw from the investigation at any time without penalty. These federally mandated requirements were not very different from the guidelines developed by the Cook Commission, except for the fact that they were now enforceable.

The National Commission conducted three-year hearings, out of which came a two-volume report, issued in 1979; *The Belmont Report: Ethical Principles and Guidelines for the Protection of Human Subjects in Research.* The Belmont Report recommended that three basic principles—beneficence, respect, and justice—be the foundation for guidelines on research ethics. *Beneficence* means that any potential harm to research participants should be minimized and any benefits maximized. *Respect* means that we are individually responsible for protecting the rights, freedom, and dignity of our participants. *Justice* means that the benefits of research should accrue equitably, and that the risks of research should be borne equitably, across different segments of society. Beneficence, respect, and justice promise to become the watchwords of ethical guidelines in behavioral and social science in the years ahead.

Where Are We Heading?

Since the 1970s, IRBs have expanded their sphere of responsibility because of a proliferation of self-imposed safeguards, legally mandated constraints, pressures by advocacy groups, and methodological developments.[52] In many cases, the responsibility of IRBs is no longer limited to the evaluation of grant submissions but encompasses *any* proposed study in the institution. Not many years ago, IRBs were regarded as the guardians of informed consent, confidentiality, and the safety and autonomy of the research participants. Today, some IRBs, particularly in medical schools, routinely evaluate technical criteria, including various design and statistical features.[53]

As if the pursuit of science were not already complicated enough, there are also state laws that limit the degree of acceptable risk to the research participants, which imply that some IRBs are legally bound to impose stricter standards.[54] Not surprisingly, the result could be that a research proposal approved without alterations at one institution may be summarily rejected at another institution.[55] This problem of variability in decision making may be compounded by the very subjectivity of the review process and the specific composition of different review boards.

In this vein, Allan J. Kimmel discovered that certain biases in ethical decision making involving human participant research correlated with biographical factors.[56] Using psychologists as judges in a survey study, Kimmel found that those who tended to be more approving in their ethical judgments were more often men, had held a Ph.D. for a longer time, had received this degree in a basic psychology area (e.g., social, experimental, or developmental), and were employed in a research-oriented context. By contrast, those who were more disapproving in their ethical judgments were more often women; had held a Ph.D. for a shorter time; had received it in counseling, school, community psychology, or some related area; and were employed in a service-oriented context. Kimmel raised the possibility of predictable biases in IRBs.

Risks and Benefits

How can researchers forearm themselves against a capricious or overly cautious ethical review? There is no simple answer to this question, but it is clear that we need to sharpen our understanding of the review process, including problems related to ethical risk-benefit decisions. Figure 6.1 shows a decision-plane model that we proposed some years ago to represent the risk-benefit process.[57] In

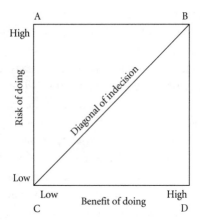

Figure 6.1 Decision-plane model representing the risk-benefit assessment process.

theory, studies falling at A will *not* be approved because the risks are high and the benefits are low; studies falling at D *will* be approved because the risks are low and the benefits are high. Studies falling along the B–C axis appear to be too difficult to decide on because the risks and benefits are equal. In the case of low-risk, low-benefit research, the IRB may be reluctant to approve a study that is harmless but is likely to yield little benefit. High-risk, high-benefit research will cause the most concern. Experienced investigators, anticipating this process, will maximize the benefits and minimize the risks as they plan their studies.

As many researchers have learned from experience, the review process often ignores benefits and merely uses the "risk of doing" for the criterion. But even when benefits are considered, the model is insufficient because it focuses only on *doing* research and ignores the costs of *not doing* research. Seldom does an IRB give any consideration to the ethical implications of failure to conduct potentially important but sensitive studies. For example, turning down a biomedical proposal that has a chance of finding a cure for AIDS but whose procedure is unable to protect the privacy of the sexual partners of the persons involved might also be evaluated on ethical grounds. Similarly, rejecting a psychological study that appears to have a chance of reducing sexism, violence, or prejudice but involves a disguised experiment in a naturalistic setting does not solve the ethical problem of passive deception and has merely traded one moral issue for another. The idea of lost opportunities has been expressed with great eloquence by John Kaplan; the context of his remarks was the use of animals in research and the efforts of "animal rights" activists to chip away "at our ability to afford animal research. . . . It is impossible to know the costs of experiments not done or research not undertaken. Who speaks for the sick, for those in pain, and for the future?"[58] In these cases, the risks of failing to conduct the research accrue to future generations or to present generations not including the research participants themselves.

Sometimes there are incidental benefits to participants that are so important that they should be considered in the calculus of the benefits. One of us was asked once to testify to an IRB about the implications of the experimenter-expectancy research for the ethics of a proposed project on karyotype presence of the XYY chromosome, which had been hypothesized to be associated with criminal behavior.[59] The tested youngsters, who were primarily of low-income families, would be followed up until adulthood so that the correlation between chromosome type and criminal behavior could be determined, with all the children to be given free, high-quality pediatric care for 20 years. It was feared, however, that if the research were not done double-blind, the parents' or researchers' expectations of increased criminal behavior by the XYY males might become a self-fulfilling prophecy. Although a double-blind study should have solved that problem, the IRB decided not to permit the research anyway. The IRB did not consider the enormous cost to the research participants of the study's not being done; each child lost 20 years of free, high-quality pediatric care. Was it ethically defensible to deprive scores or hundreds of low-income children of medical care they would otherwise not receive by preventing a double-blind design that had very little potential for actually harming the participants? At the very least, the risks of failing to do such research should have received full discussion, but they did not.

Waste Not, Want Not

The behavioral sciences have come a long way from the moral neutrality illusion of the "see no evil, hear no evil" era of positivistic science. As philosopher John Atwell cautioned, behavioral researchers really have no choice but to acknowledge that human participant research forces them "to tread on thin moral ice" because they are constantly in danger of violating someone's basic right, if only the right to privacy.[60] This situation promises to become more tangled in the years ahead as new issues emerge. Because research participants are precious resources—not to be squandered in badly designed, carelessly executed, poorly analyzed, or misleadingly reported studies—we urge a waste not, want not ethos. Poor quality of research design, careless execution, improper data analysis, and poorly reported results all lessen the ethical justification of any type of research project. If because of the poor quality of the science no good can come of a research study, how are we to justify the use of participants' time, attention, and effort, as well as the money, space, supplies, and other resources, that will be expended on the research project?[61]

We began this book with one metaphorical theme, and we will end with another. Isaiah Berlin once drew on a line from the Greek poet Archilochus to illustrate two worldviews: "The fox knows many things, but the hedgehog knows one big thing."[62] A generation or more ago, behavioral and social researchers were as yet unencumbered by the tough ethical questions that confront new researchers today. The pursuit of science in virtually all disciplines belonged to the hedgehogs, with their single central vision of science as, in the words of Gerald Holton, an "endless frontier."[63] However, this generation of researchers has been handed an "ideology of limits"[64]—laid down in self-imposed and legally mandated constraints, and overseen by the IRBs that peer over our shoulders. Given the diverse and everchanging montage of values and dilemmas, science will have little room for researchers with reduced attention spans, one-track minds, or self-serving orientations. Clearly, much is at stake when researchers are caught in a struggle with conflicting values. The future of behavioral science belongs to those researchers who can pursue different ends, often contradictory, and work on several levels simultaneously. The rise of behavioral science took root in the dreams and efforts of scientific hedgehogs, but the future of our science belongs to the foxes.

Notes

Epigraph

1. From O. Neurath, *Antispengler,* translated by Trude Parzen (Munich: Callwey, 1921), pp. 75–76.

Chapter 1

1. Quoted from p. 4 in H. H. Hyman, *Interviewing in Social Research* (Chicago, University of Chicago Press, 1954).

2. Quoted from p. 13 in W. J. McGuire, "Suspiciousness of Experimenter's Intent," in R. Rosenthal and R. L. Rosnow (Eds.), *Artifact in Behavioral Research* (New York: Academic Press, 1969), pp. 13–57.

3. See O. Pfungst, *Clever Hans (The Horse of Mr. von Osten),* edited with an introduction by Robert Rosenthal (New York: Holt, Rinehart & Winston, 1965), first published by Holt, 1911.

4. The term *Hawthorne effect* was coined by J. R. P. French in his chapter "Experiments in Field Settings," in L. Festinger and D. Katz's *Research Methods in the Behavioral Sciences* (New York: Holt, 1953), pp. 267–269.

5. Described in F. J. Roethlisberger and W. J. Dickson's *Management and the Worker* (Cambridge: Harvard University Press, 1939).

6. See R. Gillespie, "The Hawthorne Experiments and the Politics of Experimentation," in J. G. Morawski (Ed.), *The Rise of Experimentation in American Psychology* (New Haven: Yale University Press, 1988), pp. 114–137.

7. Gillespie, ibid., p. 121.

8. See, e.g., Gillespie, ibid.; R. H. Franke and J. D. Kaul, "The Hawthorne Experiments: First Statistical Interpretation," *American Sociological Review,* 1978, vol. 43, pp. 623–643; R. Schlaifer, "The Relay Assembly Test Room: An Alternative Statistical Interpretation," *American Sociological Review,* 1980, vol. 45, pp. 995–1005;

D. Bramel and R. Friend, "Hawthorne, the Myth of the Docile Worker, and Class Bias in Psychology," *American Psychologist,* 1981, vol. 36, pp. 867–878; J. Adair, "The Hawthorne Effect: A Reconsideration of the Methodological Artifact," *Journal of Applied Psychology,* 1984, vol. 69, pp. 334–345.

9. This perspective has been discussed by H. M. Parsons in a number of articles and chapters, including "What Happened at Hawthorne," *Science,* 1974, vol. 183, pp. 922–932; "What Caused the Hawthorne Effect? A Scientific Detective Story," *Administration and Society,* 1978, vol. 10, pp. 259–283; and "Assembly Ergonomics in the Hawthorne Studies," in M. Helander and M. Nagamachi (Eds.), *Design for Manufacturability: A Systems Approach to Concurrent Engineering and Ergonomics* (London: Taylor & Francis, 1992), pp. 244–253.

10. See R. Sommer, "Hawthorne Dogma," *Psychological Bulletin,* 1968, vol. 70, pp. 592–595.

11. That is, the nature of such an effect is uncertain, as there may be a positive change in behavior (as the researchers in the Hawthorne study claimed), a negative change (as others have reported), or even no change at all. See, e.g., Sommer, "Hawthorne Dogma," op. cit.; R. L. Dipboye and M. F. Flanagan, "Research Findings in the Field More Generalizable Than in the Laboratory?" *American Psychologist,* 1979, vol. 34, pp. 141–150; V. E. O'Leary, "The Hawthorne Effect in Reverse: Trainee Orientation for the Hard-Core Unemployed Woman," *Journal of Applied Psychology,* 1972, vol. 56, pp. 491–494.

12. S. Rosenzweig, "The Experimental Situation as a Psychological Problem," *Psychological Review,* 1933, vol. 40, pp. 337–354.

13. See, e.g., L. J. Stricker, "The True Deceiver," *Psychological Bulletin,* 1967, vol. 68, pp. 13–20.

14. Once researchers realized the existence of artifacts, they also sometimes overemphasized the presence of artifacts and scared themselves silly. Some jumped to the conclusion that animals were invariably better as subjects because they did not know the difference between an experiment and real life. But Clever Hans sought to please and, even though ignorant of the implications drawn by the observers, became a source of subject artifacts.

15. See J. Kihlstrom, "On the Validity of Psychology Experiments," *APS Observer,* 1995, vol. 8, no. 5, pp. 10–11.

16. Quoted from Hyman, op. cit.

17. See discussions by J. M. Suls and R. L. Rosnow, "The Delicate Balance between Ethics and Artifacts in Behavioral Research," in A. J. Kimmel

(Ed.), *Ethics of Human Subject Research* (San Francisco: Jossey-Bass, 1981), pp. 55–67; J. M. Suls and R. L. Rosnow, "Concerns about Artifacts in Psychological Experiments," in J. G. Morawski (Ed.), *The Rise of Experimentation in American Psychology* (New Haven: Yale University Press, 1988), pp. 163–187.

18. This quote—from p. 163 in J. B. Watson, "Psychology as a Behaviorist Views It," *Psychological Review*, 1913, vol. 20, pp. 158–177—was taken from a secondary source: J. G. Adair's *The Human Subject: The Social Psychology of the Psychological Experiment* (Boston: Little, Brown, 1973).

19. Ibid.

20. For a discussion, see S. Toulmin and D. E. Leary, "The Cult of Empiricism in Psychology, and Beyond," in S. Koch and D. E. Leary (Eds.), *A Century of Psychology as a Science: Retrospections and Assessment* (New York: McGraw-Hill, 1985), pp. 594–617.

21. See pp. 18–19 in I. Silverman, *The Human Subject in the Psychological Laboratory* (New York: Pergamon, 1977).

22. A. Comte, *The Essential Comte: Selected from Cours de Philosophie Positive* (New York: Barnes & Noble, 1974), first published 1830–1842.

23. For a discussion of the human subject's changing role in the history of psychology, see, e.g., D. P. Schultz, "The Human Subject in Psychological Research," *Psychological Bulletin*, 1969, vol. 72, pp. 214–228; J. G. Adair, *The Human Subject*, op. cit.).

24. See p. xi in Silverman, *The Human Subject in the Psychological Laboratory*, op. cit.

25. Quoted from p. 6 in S. M. Jourard, "A Humanistic Revolution in Psychology," reprinted in A. G. Miller (Ed.), *The Social Psychology of Psychological Research* (New York: Free Press, 1972), pp. 6–13.

Chapter 2

1. Quoted from p. ix in W. I. B. Beveridge, *The Art of Scientific Investigation*, 3rd ed. (New York: Vintage Books, 1957).

2. E. Morin, *Rumor in Orléans* (New York: Pantheon, 1971).

3. See, e.g., R. L. Rosnow, "Inside Rumors: A Personal Journey," *American Psychologist*, 1991, vol. 46, pp. 484–496.

4. D. M. Johnson, "The 'Phantom Anesthetist' of Mattoon: A Field Study of Hysteria," *Journal of Abnormal and Social Psychology*, 1945, vol. 30, pp. 175–186.

5. R. P. Feynman, *"What Do You Care What Other People Think?" Further Adventures of a Curious Character* (New York: Bantam Books, 1989), pp. 146–157.

6. Ibid., p. 147.

7. Ibid.

8. F. W. Lane, *Kingdom of the Octopus* (New York: Sheridan House, 1960).

9. M. L. Johnson, "Seeing's Believing," *New Biology*, 1953, vol. 15, pp. 60–80.

10. Ibid., p. 79.

11. Reported in R. Rosenthal, "Interpersonal Expectations," in R. Rosenthal and R. L. Rosnow (Eds.), *Artifact in Behavioral Research* (New York: Academic Press, 1969).

12. Many examples of this and other effects discussed in this chapter can be found in R. Rosenthal's *Experimenter Effects in Behavioral Research* (New York: Appleton-Century-Crofts, 1966); see also the enlarged edition of this book, published by Irvington Press in 1976.

13. M. Polanyi, *Personal Knowledge* (Chicago: University of Chicago Press, 1958).

14. A. Koestler, *The Act of Creation* (New York: Macmillan, 1964).

15. J. J. Sherwood and M. Nataupsky, "Predicting the Conclusions of Negro-White Intelligence Research from Biographical Characteristics of the Investigator," *Journal of Personality and Social Psychology*, 1968, vol. 8, pp. 53–58.

16. See, e.g., R. L. Rosnow and R. Rosenthal, "Computing Contrasts, Effect Sizes, and Counternulls on Other People's Published Data: General Procedures for Research Consumers," *Psychological Methods*, 1996, vol. 1, pp. 331–340.

17. Quoted from L. P. Williams, "The Beringer Hoax," *Science*, 1963, vol. 140, p. 1083.

18. M. E. Jahn and D. J. Woolf (Eds.), *The Lying Stones of Dr. Johann Bartholomew Adam Beringer, Being his Lithographiae Wirceburgensis* (Berkeley: University of California Press, 1963).

19. H. H. Hyman, W. J. Cobb, J. J. Feldman, C. W. Hart, and C. H. Stember, *Interviewing in Social Research* (Chicago: University of Chicago Press, 1954).

20. See also D. Calahan, V. Tamulonis, and H. W. Verner, "Interviewer Bias Involved in Certain Types of Opinion Survey Questions," *International Journal of Opinion and Attitude Research*, 1947, vol. 1, pp. 63–77; Leo P. Crespi, "The Cheater Problem in Polling," *Public Opinion Quarterly*, 1945–1946, vol. 9, pp. 421–445; P. C. Mahalanobis, "Recent Experiments in Statistical Sampling in the Indian Statistical Institute," *Journal of the Royal Statistical Society*, 1946, vol. 109, pp. 325–370.

21. See discussions in N. Wade, "IQ and Heredity: Suspicion of Fraud Beclouds Classic Experiment," *Science,* 1976, vol. 194, pp. 916–919; L. S. Hearnshaw, *Cyril Burt, Psychologist* (Ithaca, NY: Cornell University Press, 1979); D. D. Dorfman, "The Cyril Burt Question: New Findings," *Science,* 1978, vol. 201, pp. 1177–1186.

22. L. Kamin, *The Science and Politics of IQ* (Potomac, MD: Erlbaum, 1974).

23. O. Gillie, "Burt's Missing Ladies," *Science,* 1979, vol. 204, pp. 1025–1039; see also O. Gillie, "Sir Cyril Burt and the Great IQ Fraud," *New Statesman,* November 24, 1978, pp. 688–694.

24. See also discussions by A. R. Jensen, "Sir Cyril Burt in Perspective," *American Psychologist,* 1978, vol. 33, pp. 499–503; M. McAskie, "Carelessness or Fraud in Sir Cyril Burt's Kinship Data? A Critique of Jensen's Analysis," *American Psychologist,* 1978, vol. 33, pp. 496–498; D. Cohen, "British Society Takes Stand on Burt; Tackles Practical Problems," *APA Monitor,* 1980, vol. 11, no. 5, pp. 1, 9.

25. This example was taken from D. T. Campbell and J. C. Stanley, *Experimental and Quasi-Experimental Designs for Research* (Chicago: Rand McNally, 1963).

26. R. E. Lana, "Pretest Sensitization," in R. Rosenthal and R. L. Rosnow (Eds.), *Artifact in Behavioral Research* (New York: Academic Press, 1969), pp. 119–141. See also M. J. Mahoney, *Scientist as Subject: The Psychological Imperative* (Cambridge, MA: Ballinger, 1976), p. 163.

27. Lana, ibid. See also pp. 104–105 in W. Heisenberg, *Physics and Philosophy* (New York: Harper Torchbooks, 1958).

28. R. Christie, "Experimental Naivete and Experiential Naivete," *Psychological Bulletin,* 1951, vol. 48, pp. 327–339.

29. W. H. Gantt, "Autonomic Conditioning," in J. Wolpe, A. Salter, and L. J. Reyna (Eds.), *The Conditioning Therapies* (New York: Holt, Rinehart, & Winston, 1964), pp. 115–126.

30. Rosenthal, *Experimenter Effects in Behavioral Research,* ibid. See also K. J. Gergen, A. Gulerce, A. Lock, and G. Misra, "Psychological Science in Cultural Context," *American Psychologist,* 1996, vol. 51, pp. 496–503.

31. Rosenthal, ibid. Also, e.g., M. Gall and G. A. Mendelsohn, *Effects of Facilitating Techniques and Subject-Experimenter Interaction on Creative Problem Solving,* unpublished manuscript, University of California, Berkeley, 1966; V. J. Cieutat, "Examiner Differences with the Stanford-Binet IQ," *Perceptual and Motor Skills,* 1965, vol. 20, pp. 317–318; V. J. Cieutat and G. L. Flick, "Examiner Differences among Stanford-Binet Items," *Psychological Reports,* 1967, vol. 21, pp. 613–622; B. L. Kintz, D. J. Delprato, D. R. Mettee, C. E. Parsons, and R. H. Schappe, "The Experimenter as a

Discriminative Stimulus in a T-Maze," *Psychological Record*, 1965, vol. 15, pp. 449–454.

32. See R. Rosenthal, "Covert Communication in the Psychological Experiment," *Psychological Bulletin*, 1966, vol. 67, pp. 356–367.

33. See, e.g., Rosenthal, *Experimenter Effects in Behavioral Research*, op. cit.; J. L. Shapiro, *The Effects of Sex, Instructional Set, and the Problem of Awareness in a Verbal Conditioning Paradigm*, master's thesis, Northwestern University, 1966.

34. Rosenthal, *Experimenter Effects in Behavioral Research*, op. cit.

35. Ibid.

36. Ibid.

37. D. P. Crowne and D. Marlowe, *The Approval Motive* (New York: Wiley, 1964).

38. Rosenthal, *Experimenter Effects in Behavioral Research*, ibid.

39. A. P. Towbin, "Hostility in Rorschach Content and Overt Aggressive Behavior," *Journal of Abnormal and Social Psychology*, 1959, vol. 58, pp. 312–316.

40. R. E. Walker, W. E. Davis, and A. Firetto, "An Experimenter Variable: The Psychologist-Clergyman," *Psychological Reports*, 1968, vol. 22, pp. 709–714.

41. While this study showed no simple effect of being contacted by a priest as opposed to a layman, an earlier study did show such differences. See R. E. Walker and A. Firetto, "The Clergyman as a Variable in Psychological Testing," *Journal for the Scientific Study of Religion*, 1965, vol. 4, pp. 234–236.

42. See, e.g., W. C. Engram, *One Aspect of the Social Psychology of Experimentation: The E Effect and Related Personality Characteristics in the Experimenter*, doctoral dissertation, Cornell University, 1966.

43. R. A. Goldblatt and R. A. Schackner, *Categorizing Emotion Depicted in Facial Expressions and Reaction to the Experimental Situation as a Function of Experimenter Friendliness*, paper presented at the meeting of the Eastern Psychological Association, Washington, DC, April 1968.

44. R. B. Malmo, T. J. Boag, and A. A. Smith, "Physiological Study of Personal Interaction," *Psychosomatic Medicine*, 1957, vol. 19, pp. 105–119.

45. Rosenthal, *Experimenter Effects in Behavioral Research*, op. cit.

46. S. M. Jourard, *Project Replication: Experimenter-Subject Acquaintance and Outcome in Psychological Research*, unpublished manuscript, University of Florida, 1968.

47. E. L. Sacks, "Intelligence Scores as a Function of Experimentally Established Social Relationships between Child and Examiner," *Journal of Abnormal and Social Psychology,* 1952, vol. 47, pp. 354–358.

48. Rosenthal, *Experimenter Effects in Behavioral Research,* ibid.

49. See, e.g., R. Rosenthal, P. Kohn, P. M. Greenfield, and N. Carota, "Experimenters' Hypothesis-Confirmation and Mood as Determinants of Experimental Results," *Perceptual and Motor Skills,* 1965, vol. 20, pp. 1237–1252; also Rosenthal, *Experimenter Effects in Behavioral Research,* op. cit.

50. R. Rosenthal, *Experimenter Effects in Behavioral Research,* op. cit.

51. H. W. Riecken, "A Program for Research on Experiments in Social Psychology," in N. F. Washburne (Ed.), *Decisions, Values, and Groups,* vol. 2 (New York: Pergamon Press, 1962).

52. R. Sommer, "Hawthorne Dogma," *Psychological Bulletin,* 1968, vol. 70, pp. 592–595.

53. H. B. Hovey, "Effects of General Distraction on the Higher Thought Processes," *American Journal of Psychology,* 1928, vol. 40, pp. 585–591.

54. See Hyman et al., *Interviewing in Social Research,* op. cit.; E. E. Maccoby and N. Maccoby, "The Interview: A Tool of Social Science," in G. Lindzey (Ed.), *Handbook of Social Psychology,* vol. 1 (Cambridge, MA: Addison-Wesley, 1954), pp. 449–487.

55. R. Rosenthal, "Experimenter Modeling Effects as Determinants of Subject's Responses," *Journal of Projective Techniques and Personality Assessment,* 1963, vol. 27, pp. 467–471.

56. Hyman et al., *Interviewing in Social Research,* op. cit.

57. S. R. Graham, "The Influence of Therapist Character Structure upon Rorschach Changes in the Course of Psychotherapy," *American Psychologist,* 1960, vol. 15, p. 415. (Abstract)

58. Further evidence for modeling by the therapist comes from the work of Bandura, Lipsher, and Miller, who found that more directly hostile therapists were more likely to approach their patients' hostility, whereas less directly hostile therapists tended to avoid their patients' hostility. The approach or avoidance of the hostile material, then, tended to determine the patient's subsequent dealing with topics involving hostility. Not surprisingly, when therapists tended to avoid the topic, patients tended to drop it as well. See A. Bandura, D. H. Lipsher, and P. E. Miller, "Psychotherapists' Approach-Avoidance Reactions to Patients' Expression of Hostility," *American Psychologist,* 1959, vol. 14, p. 335 (Abstract).

59. P. Cook-Marquis, *Authoritarian or Acquiescent: Some Behavioral Differences,* paper presented at the American Psychological Association meeting, Washington, DC, September 1958.

60. P. G. Barnard, *Interaction Effects among Certain Experimenter and Subject Characteristics on a Projective Test,* doctoral dissertation, University of Washington, 1963.

61. F. H. Allport, *Theories of Perception and the Concept of Structure* (New York: Wiley, 1955).

62. The studies and their particular correlations were as follows: A correlation of +.52 ($N = 10$ experimenters) was found by R. Rosenthal and K. L. Fode, "(Psychology of the Scientist: V) Three Experiments in Experimenter Bias," *Psychological Reports,* 1963, vol. 12, pp. 491–511. A correlation of +.65 ($N = 24$) was reported by Hinkel (personal communication to Rosenthal, 1961). A correlation of +.18 ($N = 12$) was reported by R. Rosenthal, G. W. Persinger, L. Vikan-Kline, and K. Fode, "The Effect of Early Data Returns on Data Subsequently Obtained by Outcome-Biased Experimenters," *Sociometry,* 1963, vol. 26, pp. 487–498. A correlation of +.31 ($N = 18$) was reported by R. Rosenthal, G. W. Persinger, L. Vikan-Kline, and K. L. Fode, "The Effect of Experimenter-Outcome Bias and Subject Set on Awareness in Verbal Conditioning Experiments," *Journal of Verbal Learning and Verbal Behavior,* 1963, vol. 2, pp. 275–283. A correlation of –.07 ($N = 18$) was reported by C. R. White, *The Effect of Induced Subject Expectations on the Experimenter Bias Situation,* doctoral dissertation, University of North Dakota, 1962. A correlation of –.32 ($N = 26$) was reported by R. Rosenthal, G. W. Persinger, L. Vikan-Kline, and R. C. Mulry, "The Role of the Research Assistant in the Mediation of Experimenter Bias," *Journal of Personality,* 1963, vol. 31, pp. 313–335. A correlation of –.49 ($N = 12$) was reported by G. W. Persinger, *The Effect of Acquaintanceship on the Mediation of Experimenter Bias,* unpublished master's thesis, University of North Dakota, 1962. A correlation of +.14 ($N = 25$) was reported in both R. Rosenthal, G. W. Persinger, R. C. Mulry, L. Vikan-Kline, and M. Grothe, "Changes in Experimental Hypotheses as Determinants of Experimental Results," *Journal of Projective Techniques and Personality Assessment,* 1964, vol. 28, pp. 465–469, and "Emphasis on Experimental Procedure, Sex of Subjects, and the Biasing Effects of Experimental Hypotheses," *Journal of Projective Techniques and Personality Assessment,* 1964, vol. 28, pp. 470–473. Correlations in two studies of –.18 ($N = 9$) and +.54 ($N = 7$) were reported by Haley and Rosenthal in an unpublished manuscript, 1964.

63. See Rosenthal, *Experimenter Effects in Behavioral Research,* op. cit.

64. In survey research, modeling effects tend to be in the expected direction and to be variable in magnitude. In laboratory studies, modeling effects are variable not only in magnitude but also in direction. In the studies noted above, the correlations ranged from +.65 to −.49 between the student experimenters' own ratings of the photos and the mean ratings they subsequently obtained from their participants. The interpretation of the variability of direction of modeling effects that is best supported by the evidence is that a negative correlation is likely when the experimenter is a happier, more pleasant, less tense individual, and that a positive correlation is likely when the experimenter is a less pleasant, more tense individual. Just why that should be is not at all clear.

65. K. Pearson, "On the Mathematical Theory of Errors of Judgment with Special Reference to the Personal Equation," *Philosophical Transactions of the Royal Society of London,* 1902, vol. 198, pp. 235–299.

66. Quote taken from L. W. Hurvich's "Hering and the Scientific Establishment," *American Psychologist,* 1969, vol. 24, pp. 497–514. For an example of Lavoisier's crease in the area of data analysis, see R. L. Rosnow and R. Rosenthal, "Contrasts and Interactions Redux: Five Easy Pieces," *Psychological Science,* 1996, vol. 7, pp. 253–257.

67. K. R. Popper, *Logik der Forschung* (Vienna: Springer-Verlag, 1934).

68. F. W. Lane, *Kingdom of the Octopus,* op. cit.

69. See also L. Wolins, "Responsibility for Raw Data," *American Psychologist,* 1962, vol. 17, pp. 657–658.

70. Example from p. xii in J. B. Conant, "Introduction," in J. B. Conant and L. K. Nash (Eds.), *Harvard Case Studies in Experimental Science,* vol. 1 (Cambridge: Harvard University Press, 1957), pp. vii–xvi.

71. An additional problem in behavioral research is a confusion about the meaning of "successful replication." Elsewhere we have discussed the frequent situation in which replications are very successful in obtaining similar effect sizes but are erroneously considered unsuccessful because one result is "significant" while the other result is not. See, e.g., R. Rosenthal and R. L. Rosnow, *Essentials of Behavioral Research: Methods and Data Analysis* (New York: McGraw-Hill, 1991); R. Rosenthal, "Progress in Clinical Psychology: Is There Any?" *Clinical Psychology: Science and Practice,* 1995, vol. 2, pp. 133–150.

Chapter 3

1. Quoted from p. 138 in A. Kaplan, *The Conduct of Inquiry: Methodology for Behavioral Science* (Scranton, PA: Chandler, 1964).

2. See N. Z. Medalia and O. N. Larsen, "Diffusion and Belief in a Collective Delusion: The Seattle Windshield Pitting Epidemic," *American Sociological Review,* 1958, vol. 23, pp. 180–186.

3. See, e.g., R. L. Rosnow and G. A. Fine, *Rumor and Gossip: The Social Psychology of Hearsay* (New York: Elsevier, 1976).

4. R. K. Merton, "The Self-Fulfilling Prophecy," *Antioch Review,* 1948, vol. 8, pp. 193–210.

5. Ibid., p. 195.

6. G. W. Allport, "The Role of Expectancy," in H. Cantril (Ed.), *Tensions That Cause Wars* (Urbana: University of Illinois Press, 1950), pp. 43–78.

7. K. B. Clark, "Educational Stimulation of Racially Disadvantaged Children," in A. H. Passow (Ed.), *Education in Depressed Areas* (New York: Bureau of Publications, Columbia University, 1963), pp. 142–162.

8. For a more detailed discussion, see the chapter by Rosenthal, "Interpersonal Expectations: Some Antecedents and Some Consequences," in P. D. Blanck (Ed.), *Interpersonal Expectations: Theory, Research, and Applications* (Cambridge, UK: Cambridge University Press, 1993).

9. R. Rosenthal and K. L. Fode, "The Problem of Experimenter Outcome-Bias," in D. P. Ray (Ed.), *Series Research in Social Psychology* (Washington, DC: National Institute of Social and Behavioral Science, 1961).

10. R. Rosenthal and K. L. Fode, "The Effect of Experimenter Bias on the Performance of the Albino Rat," *Behavioral Science,* 1963, vol. 8, pp. 183–189.

11. R. Rosenthal and R. Lawson, "A Longitudinal Study of the Effects of Experimenter Bias on the Operant Conditioning of Laboratory Rats," *Journal of Psychiatric Research,* 1964, vol. 2, pp. 61–72.

12. Letter dated November 18, 1963, to Rosenthal; see R. Rosenthal, "Interpersonal Expectations: Some Antecedents and Some Consequences," in P. D. Blanck (Ed.), *Interpersonal Expectations: Theory, Research, and Applications,* op. cit., p. 9.

13. R. Rosenthal and L. Jacobson, *Pygmalion in the Classroom: Teacher Expectation and Pupils' Intellectual Development* (New York: Holt, Rinehart & Winston, 1968); expanded edition published by Irvington, New York, 1992.

14. See, e.g., P. D. Blanck, "Calibrating the Scales of Justice: Studying Judges' Behavior in Jury and Bench Trials," *Indiana Law Journal,* 1993, vol. 68, no. 4, pp. 1119–1198; P. D. Blanck, "Interpersonal Expectations in the Courtroom: Studying Judges' and Juries' Behavior," in P. D. Blanck (Ed.), *Interpersonal Expectations: Theory, Research, and Applications* (Cambridge: Cambridge University Press, 1993), pp. 64–87.

15. See, e.g., M. C. Taylor, "Race, Sex, and the Expression of Self-fulfilling Prophecies in a Laboratory Teaching Situation," *Journal of Personality and Social Psychology,* 1979, vol. 37, pp. 897–912; M. C. Taylor, "The Perpetuation of Racial Inequality," in Blanck (Ed.), *Interpersonal Expectations: Theory, Research, and Applications,* op. cit., pp. 88–124.

16. See, e.g., D. Eden, *Pygmalion in Management: Productivity as a Self-Fulfilling Prophecy* (Lexington, MA: Lexington Books, 1990); D. Eden, "Interpersonal Expectations in Organizations," in Blanck (Ed.), *Interpersonal Expectations: Theory, Research, and Applications,* op. cit., pp. 154–178.

17. See, e.g., H. S. Friedman, *The Self-Healing Personality: Why Some People Achieve Health and Others Succumb to Illness* (New York: Holt, 1991); H. S. Friedman, "Interpersonal Expectations and the Maintenance of Health," in Blanck (Ed.), *Interpersonal Expectations: Theory, Research, and Applications,* op. cit., pp. 179–193; M. R. DiMatteo, *The Psychology of Health, Illness, and Medical Care: An Individual Perspective* (Pacific Grove, CA: Brooks/Cole, 1991); M. R. DiMatteo, "Expectations in the Physician-Patient Relationship: Implications for Patient Adherence to Medical Treatment Recommendations," in Blanck (Ed.), *Interpersonal Expectations: Theory, Research, and Applications,* op. cit., pp. 296–315.

18. See discussion by E. Babad, "Pygmalion—25 Years after Interpersonal Expectations in the Classroom," in Blanck (Ed.), *Interpersonal Expectations: Theory, Research, and Applications,* op. cit., pp. 125–153.

19. R. Rosenthal and D. B. Rubin, "Interpersonal Expectancy Effects: The First 345 Studies," *Behavioral and Brain Sciences,* 1978, vol. 3, pp. 377–415. This paper was accompanied by an open peer commentary and Rosenthal and Rubin's response to those comments. For more details about the meta-analysis in this article, see R. Rosenthal, *Meta-analytic Procedures for Social Research,* rev. ed. (Newbury Park, CA: Sage, 1991).

20. R. Rosenthal, "The 'File Drawer Problem' and Tolerance for Null Results," *Psychological Bulletin,* 1979, vol. 86, pp. 638–641.

21. See N. Nelson, R. Rosenthal, and R. L. Rosnow, "Interpretation of Significance Levels and Effect Sizes by Psychological Researchers," *American Psychologist,* 1986, vol. 45, pp. 775–777; M. Zuckerman, H. S. Hodgins, A. Zuckerman, and R. Rosenthal, "Contemporary Issues in the Analysis of Data: A Survey of 551 Psychologists," *Psychological Science,* 1993, vol. 4, pp. 49–53.

22. Such tables can be found in J. Cohen's *Statistical Power Analysis for the Behavioral Sciences,* 2nd ed. (Hillsdale, NJ: Erlbaum, 1988). Compact tables can also be found in R. Rosenthal and R. L. Rosnow, *Essentials of*

Behavioral Research: Methods and Data Analysis, 2nd ed. (New York: McGraw-Hill, 1991).

23. Two stratification variables were used: area of research and statistical significance of the results. For reaction time and inkblot tests, the two areas of research with fewer than 10 studies, all studies were included. For the remaining six areas, 15 studies were included for each area except for that of everyday situations, for which 20 studies were included. These studies were chosen as follows: the 5 most significant studies were included for each area except for the area of everyday situations, for which the 10 most significant studies were included, and 10 studies were selected at random from the remaining studies in each area.

24. See, e.g., E. Babad, "Pygmalion—25 Years after Interpersonal Expectations in the Classroom," op. cit.

25. S. W. Raudenbush, "Magnitude of Teacher Expectancy Effects on Pupil IQ as a Function of the Credibility of Expectancy Induction: A Synthesis of Findings from 18 Experiments," *Journal of Educational Psychology,* 1984, vol. 76, pp. 85–97; S. W. Raudenbush and A. S. Bryk, "Empirical Bayes Meta-Analysis," *Journal of Educational Statistics,* 1985, vol. 10, pp. 75–98.

26. J. M. Darley and K. C. Oleson, "Introduction to Research on Interpersonal Expectations," in Blanck (Ed.), *Interpersonal Expectations: Theory, Research, and Applications,* op. cit., pp. 45–63.

27. E. E. Jones, *Interpersonal Perception* (New York: Freeman, 1991).

28. See also R. L. Rosnow, "Whatever Happened to the Law of Primacy?" *Journal of Communication,* 1966, vol. 16, pp. 10–31.

29. M. H. Birnbaum, "Morality Judgments: Tests of an Averaging Model," *Journal of Experimental Psychology,* 1972, vol. 93, pp. 35–42; M. H. Birnbaum, "Morality Judgments: Tests of an Averaging Model with Differential Weights," *Journal of Experimental Psychology,* 1973, vol. 99, pp. 395–399; G. D. Reeder and M. B. Brewer, "A Schematic Model of Dispositional Attribution in Interpersonal Perception," *Psychological Review,* 1979, vol. 89, pp. 61–79.

30. See, e.g., R. L. Rosnow, "Poultry and Prejudice," *Psychology Today,* 1972, vol. 5, no. 10, pp. 53–56.

31. J. L. Hilton and J. M. Darley, "Constructing Other Persons: A Limit on the Effect," *Journal of Experimental Social Psychology,* 1985, vol. 21, pp. 1–18.

32. R. L. Rosnow, A. A. Skleder, M. E. Jaeger, and B. Rind, "Intelligence and the Epistemics of Interpersonal Acumen: Testing Some Implications of Gardner's Theory," *Intelligence,* 1994, vol. 19, pp. 93–116; R. L. Rosnow, A. A. Skleder, and B. Rind, "Reading Other People: A Hidden Cognitive Structure?" *General Psychologist,* 1995, vol. 31, pp. 1–10.

33. See, e.g., W. B. Swann and R. J. Ely, "A Battle of Wills: Self-Verification Versus Behavioral Confirmation," *Journal of Personality and Social Psychology,* 1984, vol. 46, pp. 1287–1302.

34. See discussions by R. Rosenthal, "Pavlov's Mice, Pfungst's Horse, and Pygmalion's PONS: Some Models for the Study of Interpersonal Expectancy Effects," in T. A. Sebeok and R. Rosenthal (Eds.), *The Clever Hans Phenomenon* (Annals of the New York Academy of Sciences, 1981, No. 364); M. J. Harris and R. Rosenthal, "Mediation of Interpersonal Expectancy Effects: 31 Meta-Analyses," *Psychological Bulletin,* 1985, vol. 97, pp. 363–386.

35. J. G. Adair and J. S. Epstein, "Verbal Cues in the Mediation of Experimenter Bias," *Psychological Reports,* 1968, vol. 22, pp. 1045–1053.

36. E. J. Zoble and R. S. Lehman, "Interaction of Subject and Experimenter Expectancy Effects in a Tone Length Discrimination Task," *Behavioral Science,* 1969, vol. 14, pp. 357–363.

37. See Harris and Rosenthal, "Mediation of Interpersonal Expectancy Effects," op. cit.

38. R. Rosenthal, *Experimenter Expectancy, Covert Communication, and Meta-analytic Methods,* presented as the Donald T. Campbell Award Address, American Psychological Association meeting, August 14, 1989 (ERIC Document TM014556).

39. L. Jussim, "Self-Fulfilling Prophecies: A Theoretical and Integrative Review," *Psychological Review,* 1986, vol. 93, pp. 429–445.

40. Rosenthal and Jacobson, *Pygmalion in the Classroom,* op. cit.; W. B. Swann, Jr. and M. Snyder, "On Translating Beliefs into Action: Theories of Ability and Their Application in an Instructional Setting," *Journal of Personality and Social Psychology,* 1980, vol. 38, pp. 879–888.

41. N. Ambady and R. Rosenthal, "Thin Slices of Expressive Behavior as Predictors of Interpersonal Consequences: A Meta-analysis," *Psychological Bulletin,* 1992, vol. 111, pp. 256–274; N. Ambady and R. Rosenthal, "Half a Minute: Predicting Teacher Evaluations from Thin Slices of Nonverbal Behavior and Physical Attractiveness," *Journal of Personality and Social Psychology,* 1993, vol. 64, pp. 431–441.

42. See S. Hechtmann and R. Rosenthal, "Teacher Sex and Nonverbal Behavior in the Teaching of Sexually Stereotyped Materials," *Journal of Applied Social Psychology,* 1991, vol. 21, pp. 446–459. This study showed the potential of affect-effort theory in helping to explain the traditional sex differences in cognitive functioning. It was found that teachers teaching verbal material to male students and teaching quantitative material to female students (the "sex-inappropriate" materials) showed greater hostility to their students in the nonverbal channels (video-

only) than did teachers teaching the "sex-appropriate" materials to these same students. These bias effects were smaller for female than for male teachers, and they were smaller for more androgynous than for more sex-typed teachers.

43. The correlation between the need-for-approval scores and arrival time was .40. See R. Rosenthal, P. Kohn, P. M. Greenfield, and N. Carota, "Experimenters' Hypothesis-Confirmation and Mood as Determinants of Experimental Results," *Perceptual and Motor Skills,* 1965, vol. 20, pp. 1237–1252.

44. J. R. Burnham, *Experimenter Bias and Lesion Labeling,* unpublished manuscript, Purdue University, 1966.

Chapter 4

1. Epigraph quoted from p. 31 in H. W. Riecken, "A Program for Research on Experiments in Social Psychology," in N. F. Washburne (Ed.), vol. 2 *Decisions, Values and Groups* (Elmsford, NY: Pergamon, 1962), pp. 25–41.

2. J.-P. Sartre, *Being and Nothingness: A Phenomenological Essay on Ontology* (New York: Washington Square Press, 1956), pp. 340 ff.

3. See, e.g., discussions in M. T. Orne, "On the Social Psychology of the Psychological Experiment: With Particular Reference to Demand Characteristics and Their Implications," *American Psychologist,* 1962, vol. 17, pp. 776–783; M. T. Orne, "Hypnosis, Motivation, and the Ecological Validity of the Psychological Experiment," in W. J. Arnold and M. M. Page (Eds.), *Nebraska Symposium on Motivation* (Lincoln: University of Nebraska Press, 1970), pp. 187–265.

4. K. Lewin, *Die Entwicklung der Experimentellen Willenpsychologie und die Psychotherapie* (Leipzig: S. Hirzel, 1929).

5. Orne, "Hypnosis, Motivation, and the Ecological Validity of the Psychological Experiment," op. cit., pp. 194 ff.

6. M. T. Orne, "The Nature of Hypnosis: Artifact and Essence," *Journal of Abnormal and Social Psychology,* 1959, vol. 58, pp. 277–299.

7. Orne, "On the Social Psychology of the Psychological Experiment," op. cit.

8. Ibid.

9. I. Silverman, "Role-Related Behavior of Subjects in Laboratory Studies of Attitude Change," *Journal of Personality and Social Psychology,* 1968, vol. 8, pp. 343–348.

10. M. M. Page, "Modification of Figure-Ground Perception as a Function of Awareness of Demand Characteristics," *Journal of Personality and Social Psychology,* 1968, vol. 9, pp. 59–66.

11. C. N. Alexander, Jr. and H. G. Weil, "Players, Persons, and Purposes: Situational Meaning and the Prisoner's Dilemma Game," *Sociometry,* 1969, vol. 32, pp. 121–144.

12. D. R. Kauffmann, "Incentive to Perform Counterattitudinal Acts: Bribe or Gold Star?" *Journal of Personality and Social Psychology,* 1971, vol. 19, pp. 82–91; M. M. Page, "Role of Demand Awareness in the Communicator Credibility Effect," *Journal of Social Psychology,* 1970, vol. 82, pp. 57–66; R. L. Rosnow, "One-Sided versus Two-Sided Communication under Indirect Awareness of Persuasive Intent," *Public Opinion Quarterly,* 1968, vol. 32, pp. 95–101; R. L. Rosnow, H. M. Holper, and A. G. Gitter, "More on the Reactive Effects of Pretesting in Attitude Research: Demand Characteristics or Subject Commitment?" *Educational and Psychological Measurement,* 1973, vol. 33, pp. 7–17; R. L. Rosnow and J. M. Suls, "Reactive Effects of Pretesting in Attitude Research," *Journal of Personality and Social Psychology,* 1970, vol. 15, pp. 338–343; S. R. Sherman, "Demand Characteristics in an Experiment on Attitude Change," *Sociometry,* 1967, vol. 30, pp. 246–260; I. Silverman and A. D. Shulman, "Effects of Hunger on Responses to Demand Characteristics in the Measurement of Persuasion," *Psychonomic Science,* 1969, vol. 15, pp. 201–202.

13. J. G. Adair, "Preexperiment Attitudes toward Psychology as a Determinant of Experimental Results: Verbal Conditioning of Aware Subjects," *Proceedings of the 78th American Psychological Association Meeting,* 1970, vol. 5, pp. 417–418; J. H. Goldstein, R. L. Rosnow, B. E. Goodstadt, and J. M. Suls, "The 'Good Subject' in Verbal Operant Conditioning Research," *Journal of Experimental Research in Personality,* 1972, vol. 6, pp. 29–33; L. H. Levy, "Awareness, Learning, and the Beneficent Subject as Expert Witness," *Journal of Personality and Social Psychology,* 1967, vol. 6, pp. 365–370; M. M. Page, "Demand Awareness and the Verbal Operant Conditioning Experiment," *Journal of Personality and Social Psychology,* 1972, vol. 23, pp. 372–378; H. A. White and D. A. Schumsky, "Prior Information and 'Awareness' in Verbal Conditioning," *Journal of Personality and Social Psychology,* 1972, vol. 24, pp. 162–165.

14. M. M. Page, "Social Psychology of a Classical Conditioning of Attitudes Experiment," *Journal of Personality and Social Psychology,* 1969, vol. 11, pp. 177–186; M. M. Page and A. R. Lumia, "Cooperation with Demand Characteristics and the Bimodal Distribution of Verbal Conditioning Data," *Psychonomic Science,* 1968, vol. 12, pp. 243–244.

15. C. N. Alexander, Jr., L. G. Zucker, and C. L. Brody, "Experimental Expectations and Autokinetic Experiences: Consistency Theories and Judgmental Convergence," *Sociometry,* 1970, vol. 33, pp. 108–122; D. K. Bruehl and D. Solar, *Clarity of Demand Characteristics in an*

Experimenter Expectancy Experiment, paper presented at the Western Psychological Association meeting, Portland, 1972.

16. W. C. Coe, "Hypnosis as Role Enactment: The Role Demand Variable," *American Journal of Clinical Hypnosis,* 1966, vol. 8, pp. 189–191; C. W. Jackson, Jr., and E. L. Kelley, "Influence of Suggestion and Subject's Prior Knowledge in Research on Sensory Deprivation," *Science,* 1962, vol. 132, pp. 211–212; M. T. Orne, "The Nature of Hypnosis: Artifact and Essence," *Journal of Abnormal and Social Psychology,* 1959, vol. 58, pp. 277–299; M. T. Orne, "Demand Characteristics and the Concept of Quasi-Controls," in R. Rosenthal and R. L. Rosnow (Eds.), *Artifact in Behavioral Research* (New York: Academic Press, 1969, pp. 143–179); M. Orne and K. E. Scheibe, "The Contribution of Nondeprivation Factors in the Production of Sensory Deprivation Effects: The Psychology of the 'Panic Button,'" *Journal of Abnormal and Social Psychology,* 1964, vol. 68, pp. 3–12; A. M. Raffetto, *Experimenter Effects on Subjects' Reported Hallucinatory Experiences under Visual and Auditory Deprivation,* paper presented at the Midwestern Psychological Association meeting, Chicago, 1968.

17. T. R. Sarbin and K. T. Chun, *A Confirmation of the Choice of Response Hypothesis in Perceptual Defense Measurement,* paper presented at the Western Psychological Association meeting, Portland, 1964.

18. J. B. Juhasz and T. R. Sarbin, "On the False Alarm Metaphor in Psychophysics," *Psychological Record,* 1966, vol. 16, pp. 323–327.

19. R. O. Kroger, "The Effects of Role Demands and Test-Cue Properties upon Personality Test Performance," *Journal of Consulting Psychology,* 1967, vol. 31, pp. 304–312.

20. W. T. McReynolds and C. Tori, "A Further Assessment of Attention-Placebo Effects and Demand Characteristics in Studies of Systematic Desensitization," *Journal of Consulting and Clinical Psychology,* 1972, vol. 38, pp. 261–264.

21. L. A. Gustafson and M. T. Orne, "Effects of Perceived Role and Role Success on the Detection of Deception," *Journal of Applied Psychology,* 1965, vol. 49, pp. 412–417; Orne, "Demand Characteristics and the Concept of Quasi-Controls," op. cit.

22. V. L. Allen, "The Effect of Knowledge of Deception on Conformity," *Journal of Social Psychology,* 1966, vol. 69, pp. 101–106; B. W. Bragg, *Effect of Knowledge of Deception on Reaction to Group Pressure,* master's thesis, University of Wisconsin, 1966; S. H. Geller and N. S. Endler, "The Effects of Subject Roles, Demand Characteristics, and Suspicion on Conformity," *Canadian Journal of Behavioral Science,* 1973, vol. 5,

pp. 46–54; R. J. Glinski, B. C. Glinski, and G. T. Slatin, "Nonnaivety Contamination in Conformity Experiments: Sources, Effects, and Implications for Control," *Journal of Personality and Social Psychology,* 1970, vol. 16, pp. 478–485; R. K. Leik, "'Irrelevant' Aspects of Stooge Behavior: Implications for Leadership Studies and Experimental Methodology," *Sociometry,* 1965, vol. 28, pp. 259–271.

23. Riecken, "A Program for Research on Experiments in Social Psychology," op. cit.

24. Quoted from p. 282 in M. J. Rosenberg, "The Conditions and Consequences of Evaluation Apprehension," in R. Rosenthal and R. L. Rosnow (Eds.), *Artifact in Behavioral Research* (New York: Academic Press, 1969, pp. 279–349).

25. L. Festinger, *A Theory of Cognitive Dissonance* (Stanford, CA: Stanford University Press, 1957).

26. See, e.g., W. J. McGuire, "Attitudes and Opinions," *Annual Review of Psychology,* 1966, vol. 17, pp. 475–514; K. E. Weick, "When Prophecy Pales: The Fate of Dissonance Theory," *Psychological Reports,* 1965, vol. 16, pp. 1261–1275; N. P. Chapanis and A. Chapanis, "Cognitive Dissonance: Five Years Later," *Psychological Bulletin,* 1964, vol. 61, pp. 1–22; I. Silverman, "In Defense of Dissonance Theory: Reply to Chapanis and Chapanis," *Psychological Bulletin,* 1964, vol. 62, pp. 205–209.

27. M. J. Rosenberg, "When Dissonance Fails: On Eliminating Evaluation Apprehension from Attitude Measurement," *Journal of Personality and Social Psychology,* 1965, vol. 1, pp. 28–42.

28. See, e.g., J. M. Carlsmith, B. E. Collins, and R. L. Helmreich, "Studies in Forced Compliance: I. The Effect of Pressure for Compliance on Attitude Change Produced by Face-to-Face Role Playing and Anonymous Essay Writing," *Journal of Personality and Social Psychology,* 1966, vol. 4, pp. 1–13.

29. See, e.g., R. Rosenthal and R. L. Rosnow (Eds.), *Artifact in Behavioral Research* (New York: Academic Press, 1969); J. Jung, *The Experimenter's Dilemma* (New York: Harper & Row, 1971); A. G. Miller (Ed.), *The Social Psychology of Psychological Research* (New York: Free Press, 1972); J. G. Adair, *The Human Subject: The Social Psychology of the Psychological Experiment* (Boston: Little, Brown, 1973); G. Gniech, *Störeffekte in psychologischen Experimenten* (Stuttgart: Kohlhammer, 1976); I. Silverman, *The Human Subject in the Psychological Laboratory* (New York: Pergamon, 1977). See also J. Masling, "Role-Related Behavior of the Subject and Psychologist and Its Effects upon Psychological Data," in D. L. Levine (Ed.), *Nebraska Symposium on Motivation* (Lincoln:

University of Nebraska Press, 1966, pp. 67–103), in which Masling cautions that some subjects are motivated not to help the experimenter but to respond perversely to ruin the experiment.

30. See S. Milgram, *Obedience to Authority: An Experimental View* (New York: Harper & Row, 1974).

31. Quoted from p. 12 in S. Milgram, *The Individual in a Social World: Essays and Experiments* (Reading, MA: Addison-Wesley, 1977). Solomon Asch's research can be found in "Effects of Group Pressure upon the Modification and Distortion of Judgments," in G. E. Swanson, T. M. Newcomb, and E. L. Hartley (Eds.), *Readings in Social Psychology* (New York: Holt, Rinehart & Winston, 1952), pp. 393–401.

32. Quoted from p. 5 in Milgram, *Obedience to Authority,* op. cit.

33. Quoted from p. 130 in Orne and Holland's article as reprinted in A. G. Miller's anthology, *The Social Psychology of Psychological Research* (New York: Free Press, 1972), pp. 122–137. The original citation of the article is M. T. Orne and C. H. Holland, "On the Ecological Validity of Laboratory Deceptions," *International Journal of Psychiatry,* 1968, vol. 6, pp. 282–293.

34. Quoted from p. 129 in Orne and Holland's reprinted paper in Miller, *The Social Psychology of Psychological Research,* op. cit.

35. S. Milgram, "Interpreting Obedience: Error and Evidence (A Reply to Orne and Holland)," in Miller, *The Social Psychology of Psychological Research,* op. cit., pp. 138–154.

36. Borrowed from L. Rosten's *The Joys of Yiddish* (New York: McGraw-Hill, 1968).

37. Quoted from p. 3 in D. T. Campbell and J. C. Stanley, *Experimental and Quasi-Experimental Designs for Research* (Chicago: Rand McNally, 1963).

38. Quoted from p. 333 in Q. McNemar, "Opinion-Attitude Methodology," *Psychological Bulletin,* 1946, vol. 43, pp. 289–374.

39. D. O. Sears, "College Sophomores in the Laboratory: Influences of a Narrow Data Base on Social Psychology's View of Human Nature," *Journal of Personality and Social Psychology,* 1986, vol. 51, pp. 515–530.

40. Quoted from p. 19 in Silverman, *The Human Subject in the Psychology Laboratory,* op. cit.

41. L. S. Aiken and R. L. Rosnow, *Role Expectations for Psychological Research Participation,* unpublished study described in R. Rosenthal and R. L. Rosnow, *The Volunteer Subject* (New York: Wiley, 1975), pp. 163–169.

42. Quoted from p. 778 in Orne, "On the Social Psychology of the Psychological Experiment," op. cit.

43. Quoted from p. 537 in S. Fillenbaum, "Prior Deception and Subsequent Experimental Performance: The 'Faithful' Subject," *Journal of Personality and Social Psychology,* 1966, vol. 4, pp. 532–537.

44. Quoted from p. 9 in H. Sigall, E. Aronson, and T. Van Hoose, "The Cooperative Subject: Myth or Reality?" *Journal of Experimental Social Psychology,* 1970, vol. 6, pp. 1–10.

45. This scaling solution was based on the most reliable responses; interested readers will find a detailed description of the data analysis in Rosenthal and Rosnow, *The Volunteer Subject,* op. cit.

46. L. S. Aiken and R. L. Rosnow, "Role Expectations for Psychological Research Participation," unpublished study described in Rosenthal and Rosnow, *The Volunteer Subject,* op. cit., pp. 163–169.

47. Quoted from p. 229 in Orne, "Hypnosis, Motivation, and the Ecological Validity of the Psychological Experiment," op. cit.

48. Quoted from p. 260 in R. L. Rosnow, "The Researcher's Worst Friend," in P. Chance and T. G. Harris (Eds.), *The Best of Psychology Today* (New York: McGraw-Hill, 1970).

49. Sigall, Aronson, and Van Hoose, "The Cooperative Subject," op. cit.

50. J. G. Adair and B. S. Schachter, "To Cooperate or to Look Good? The Subjects' and Experimenters' Perceptions of Each Others' Intentions," *Journal of Experimental Social Psychology,* 1972, vol. 8, pp. 74–85.

51. R. L. Rosnow, B. E. Goodstadt, J. M. Suls, and A. G. Gitter, "More on the Social Psychology of the Experiment: When Compliance Turns to Self-Defense," *Journal of Personality and Social Psychology,* 1973, vol. 27, pp. 337–343.

52. See J. H. Johns and H. C. Quay, "The Effect of Social Reward on Verbal Conditioning in Psychopathic and Neurotic Military Offenders," *Journal of Consulting Psychology,* 1962, vol. 26, pp. 217–220; H. C. Quay and W. A. Hunt, "Psychopathy, Neuroticism, and Verbal Conditioning," *Journal of Consulting Psychology,* 1965, vol. 29, p. 283.

53. From J. W. Brehm's reactance theory, for example, one might predict strong negativity from people who are *required* to participate (so-called captive participants). This theory asserts that, when a person's freedom of choice between two alternatives is restricted or threatened, the person will try to restore that freedom; in so doing, the alternative that suffers the restriction will gain in attraction. See J. W. Brehm, *A Theory of Psychological Reactance* (New York: Academic Press, 1966).

54. R. L. Rosnow and L. S. Aiken, "Mediation of Artifacts in Behavioral Research," *Journal of Experimental Social Psychology,* 1973, vol. 9, pp. 181–201; R. L. Rosnow and D. J. Davis, "Demand Characteristics and the Psychological Experiment," *ETC: A Review of General Semantics,* 1977, vol. 34, pp. 301–313.

55. D. B. Strohmetz and R. L. Rosnow, "A Mediational Model of Research Artifacts," in J. Brzezinski, Ed., *Probability in Theory-Building: Experimental and Non-experimental Approaches to Scientific Research in Psychology* (Amsterdam: Editions Rodopi, 1994, pp. 177–196).

56. We thank David B. Strohmetz for allowing us to sample so liberally from the paper cited in Note 55.

57. See, e.g., C. Hendrick, "Role-Taking, Role-Playing, and the Laboratory Experiment," *Personality and Social Psychology Bulletin,* 1977, vol. 3, pp. 467–478.

58. See, e.g., M. Brenner and W. Bungard, "What to Do With Social Reactivity in Psychological Experimentation?" in M. Brenner (Ed.), *Social Method and Social Life* (London: Academic Press, 1981), pp. 89–114.

59. See discussions by R. E. Lana in, e.g., "Pretest-Treatment Interaction Effects in Attitudinal Studies," *Psychological Bulletin,* 1959, vol. 56, pp. 293–300; "The Influence of the Pretest on Order Effects in Persuasive Communications," *Journal of Abnormal and Social Psychology,* 1964, vol. 69, pp. 337–341; "Pretest Sensitization," in R. Rosenthal and R. L. Rosnow (Eds.), *Artifact in Behavioral Research* (New York: Academic Press, 1969), pp. 119–141.

60. B. Rind, "Effect of Beliefs about Weather Conditons on Tipping," *Journal of Applied Social Psychology,* 1996, vol. 26, pp. 137–147.

61. A further responsibility is to ensure that published findings will not damage the participants by subjecting them to ridicule or scorn. See also D. B. Strohmetz and A. A. Skleder, "The Use of Role-play in Teaching Research Ethics: A Validation Study," *Teaching of Psychology,* 1992, vol. 19, pp. 106–108.

62. For a review, see Lana, "Pretest Sensitization," op. cit.

63. R. L. Solomon, "An Extension of Control Group Design," *Psychological Bulletin,* 1949, vol. 46, pp. 137–150.

64. D. R. Entwisle, "Interactive Effects of Pretesting," *Educational and Psychological Measurement,* 1961, vol. 21, pp. 607–620.

65. For a detailed discussion, see Chapter 7 in R. L. Rosnow and R. Rosenthal, *Beginning Behavioral Research,* 2nd ed. (Upper Saddle River, NJ: Prentice Hall, 1996).

66. Orne, "Hypnosis, Motivation, and the Ecological Validity of the Psychological Experiment," op. cit.

67. L. A. Gustafson and M. T. Orne, "Effects of Perceived Role and Role Success on the Detection of Deception," *Journal of Applied Psychology,* 1965, vol. 49, pp. 412–417.

68. J. L. Esposito, E. Agard, and R. L. Rosnow, "Can Confidentiality of Data Pay Off?" *Personality and Individual Differences,* 1984, vol. 5, pp. 477–480; cf. C. B. Thomas, J. A. Hall, F. D. Dewhirst, G. A. Fine, M. Taylor, and R. L. Rosnow, "Evaluation Apprehension, Social Desirability, and the Interpretation of Test Correlations," *Social Behavior and Personality,* 1979, vol. 7, pp. 193–197.

69. E. E. Jones and H. Sigall, "The Bogus Pipeline: A New Paradigm for Measuring Affect and Attitude," *Psychological Bulletin,* 1971, vol. 76, pp. 349–364.

70. Quoted from p. 252 in Orne, "Hypnosis, Motivation, and the Ecological Validity of the Psychological Experiment," op. cit.

71. See, e.g., Orne, "Demand Characteristics and the Concept of Quasi-Controls," op. cit.

72. See, e.g., Rosnow and Aiken, "Mediation of Artifacts in Behavioral Research," op. cit.

73. M. T. Orne, P. W. Sheehan, and F. J. Evans, "Occurrence of Posthypnotic Behavior outside the Experimental Setting," *Journal of Personality and Social Psychology,* 1968, vol. 9, pp. 189–196.

Chapter 5

1. Quoted from p. 237 in M. T. Orne, "On the Social Psychology of the Psychological Experiment: With Particular Reference to Demand Characteristics and Their Implications," in A. G. Miller (Ed.), *The Social Psychology of Psychological Research* (New York: Free Press, 1972), pp. 233–246; this article originally appeared in the *American Psychologist,* 1962, vol. 17, pp. 776–783.

2. H. K. Beecher, *Research and the Individual: Human Studies* (Boston: Little, Brown, 1970).

3. See p. 221 in M. T. Orne, "Hypnosis, Motivation, and the Ecological Validity of the Psychological Experiment," in W. J. Arnold and M. M. Page (Eds.), *Nebraska Symposium on Motivation* (Lincoln: University of Nebraska Press, 1970), pp. 187–265.

4. See, e.g., W. G. Cochran, F. Mosteller, and J. W. Tukey, "Statistical Problems of the Kinsey Report," *Journal of the American Statistical Association*, 1953, vol. 48, pp. 673–716; W. E. Deming, "On Errors in Surveys," *American Sociological Review*, 1944, vol. 9, pp. 359–369; M. H. Hansen and W. N. Hurwitz, "The Problem of Non-response in Sample Surveys," *Journal of the American Statistical Association*, 1946, vol. 41, pp. 517–529. Interestingly, although much of the interest in, and concern over, the problem of subject selection biases has been centered on human subjects, we should note that analogous interests and concerns have been expressed among investigators using animal subjects. Thus, just as the college sophomore may not be a very good model for the "typical person," so the laboratory rat may not be a very good model for the typical rodent, nor for a wild rat, nor even for another laboratory rat.

5. See, e.g., D. Scott-Jones and R. L. Rosnow, "Ethics and Mental Health Research," in H. Friedman (Ed.), *Encyclopedia of Mental Health* (San Diego: Academic Press, in press).

6. W. G. Cochran, *Sampling Techniques*, 2nd ed. (New York: Wiley, 1963).

7. D. Wechsler, *The Measurement and Appraisal of Adult Intelligence*, 4th ed. (Baltimore: Williams & Wilkins, 1958).

8. For a detailed discussion and illustrations, see pp. 9–12 in R. Rosenthal and R. L. Rosnow, *The Volunteer Subject* (New York: Wiley, 1975).

9. Discussed in detail in Rosenthal and Rosnow, ibid., and also in R. L. Rosnow and R. Rosenthal, "Volunteer Effects in Behavioral Research," in K. H. Craik, B. Kleinmuntz, R. L. Rosnow, R. Rosenthal, J. A. Cheyne, and R. H. Walters, *New Directions in Psychology*, vol. 4 (New York: Holt, Rinehart & Winston, 1970), pp. 213–277.

10. For a detailed discussion of this research evidence, see Rosenthal and Rosnow, ibid., or Rosnow and Rosenthal, ibid.

11. R. L. Rosnow and J. M. Suls, "Reactive Effects of Pretesting in Attitude Research," *Journal of Personality and Social Psychology*, 1970, vol. 15, pp. 338–343.

12. See discussion by W. J. McGuire, "The Nature of Attitudes and Attitude Change," in G. Lindzey and E. Aronson (Eds.), *Handbook of Social Psychology*, vol. 3 (Reading, MA: Addison-Wesley, 1969).

13. J. H. Goldstein, R. L. Rosnow, B. E. Goodstadt, and J. M. Suls, "The 'Good Subject' in Verbal Operant Conditioning Research," *Journal of Experimental Research in Personality*, 1972, vol. 6, pp. 29–33.

14. Questions of the pervasiveness of volunteer artifacts and other issues were raised by A. W. Kruglanski, "Much Ado about the 'Volunteer Artifacts,'" *Journal of Personality and Social Psychology*, 1973, vol. 28,

pp. 348–354. Our response appears in R. L. Rosnow and R. Rosenthal, "Taming of the Volunteer Problem: On Coping with Artifacts by Benign Neglect," *Journal of Personality and Social Psychology*, 1974, vol. 30, pp. 188–190.

15. I. A. Horowitz, "Effects of Volunteering, Fear Arousal, and Number of Communications on Attitude Change," *Journal of Personality and Social Psychology*, 1969, vol. 11, pp. 34–37.

16. H. Kotses, K. D. Glaus, and L. E. Fisher, "Effects of Subject Recruitment Procedure on Heart Rate and Skin Conductance Measures," *Biological Psychology*, 1974, vol. 2, pp. 59–66.

17. R. W. Black, J. Schumpert, and F. A. Welch, "A 'Partial Reinforcement Extinction Effect' in Perceptual-Motor Performance: Coerced versus Volunteer Subject Populations," *Journal of Experimental Psychology*, 1972, vol. 92, pp. 143–145.

18. See also, e.g., D. W. King and L. A. King, "Validity Issues in Research on Vietnam Veteran Adjustment," *Psychological Bulletin*, 1991, vol. 109, pp. 107–124; D. B. Strohmetz, A. I. Alterman, and D. Walter, "Subject Selection Bias in Alcoholics Volunteering for a Treatment Study," *Alcoholism: Clinical and Experimental Research*, 1990, vol. 14, pp. 736–738.

19. See, e.g., J. Cohen, *Statistical Power Analysis for the Behavioral Sciences*, 2nd ed. (Hillsdale, NJ: Erlbaum, 1988); H. C. Kraemer and S. Thiemann, *How Many Subjects? Statistical Power Analysis in Research* (Beverly Hills, CA: Sage, 1987); R. Rosenthal and R. L. Rosnow, *Essentials of Behavioral Research: Methods and Data Analysis*, 2nd ed. (New York: McGraw-Hill, 1991).

20. Rosenthal and Rosnow, *The Volunteer Subject*, op. cit.

21. A. H. Maslow and J. M. Sakoda, "Volunteer-Error in the Kinsey Study," *Journal of Abnormal and Social Psychology*, 1952, vol. 47, pp. 259–262.

22. A. C. Kinsey, W. B. Pomeroy, and C. E. Martin, *Sexual Behavior in the Human Male* (Philadelphia: Saunders, 1948); A. C. Kinsey, W. B. Pomeroy, C. E. Martin, and P. H. Gebhard, *Sexual Behavior in the Human Female* (Philadelphia: Saunders, 1953).

23. See, e.g., W. G. Cochran, F. Mosteller, and J. W. Tukey, "Statistical Problems of the Kinsey Report," *Journal of the American Statistical Association*, 1953, vol. 48, pp. 673–716; J. Dollard, "The Kinsey Report on Women: 'A Strangely Flawed Masterpiece,'" *New York Herald Tribune*, September 13, 1953, Section 6; H. Hyman and P. B. Sheatsley, "The Scientific Method," in D. P. Geddes (Ed.), *An Analysis of the Kinsey Reports* (New York: New American Library, 1954).

24. A. H. Maslow, "Self-esteem (Dominance Feelings) and Sexuality in Women," *Journal of Social Psychology,* 1942, vol. 16, pp. 259–293.

25. Similarly, Diamant argued that estimates of premarital sexual behavior may be inflated when only volunteer subjects are interviewed. He found college-age male volunteers more apt to report having experienced sexual intercourse than male nonvolunteers and also to be significantly more permissive than the nonvolunteers in their attitudes about sex. See L. Diamant, "Attitude, Personality, and Behavior in Volunteers and Nonvolunteers for Sexual Research," *Proceedings, 78th Annual Convention, American Psychological Association,* 1970, pp. 423–424. Similar results were reported by G. R. Kaats and K. E. Davis and by Siegman: see G. R. Kaats and K. E. Davis, "Effects of Volunteer Biases in Studies of Sexual Behavior and Attitudes," *Journal of Sex Research,* 1971, vol. 7, pp. 26–34; A. Siegman, "Responses to a Personality Questionnaire by Volunteers and Nonvolunteers to a Kinsey Interview," *Journal of Abnormal and Social Psychology,* 1956, vol. 52, pp. 280–281.

Chapter 6

1. Quoted from p. 379 in A. Kaplan, *The Conduct of Inquiry: Methodology for Behavioral Science* (Scranton, PA: Chandler, 1964).

2. See, e.g., discussions by D. T. Campbell in *Methodology and Epistemology for Social Science: Selected Papers* (Chicago: University of Chicago Press, 1988); A. C. Houts, T. D. Cook, and W. Shadish, Jr., "The Person-Situation Debate: A Critical Multiplist Perspective," *Journal of Personality,* 1986, vol. 54, pp. 52–105; M. E. Jaeger and R. L. Rosnow, "Contextualism and Its Implications for Psychological Inquiry," *British Journal of Psychology,* 1988, vol. 79, pp. 63–75; R. L. Rosnow, *Paradigms in Transition: The Methodology of Social Inquiry* (New York: Oxford University Press, 1981).

3. For further discussion, see, e.g., R. L. Rosnow and M. Georgoudi (Eds.), *Contextualism and Understanding in Behavioral Science: Implications for Research and Theory* (New York: Praeger, 1986).

4. See, e.g., A. J. Kimmel, *Ethical Issues in Behavioral Research: A Survey* (Cambridge, MA: Blackwell, 1996); R. L. Rosnow, M. J. Rotheram-Borus, S. J. Ceci, P. D. Blanck, and G. P. Koocher, "The Institutional Review Board as a Mirror of Scientific and Ethical Standards," *American Psychologist,* 1993, vol. 48, pp. 821–826.

5. See, e.g., P. D. Blanck, A. S. Bellack, R. L. Rosnow, M. J. Rotheram-Borus, and N. R. Schooler, "Scientific Rewards and Conflicts of Ethical Choices in Human Subjects Research," *American Psychologist,* 1992, vol. 47,

pp. 959–965; D. T. Campbell, "Prospective: Artifact and Control," in R. Rosenthal and R. L. Rosnow (Eds.), *Artifact in Behavioral Research* (New York: Academic Press, 1969), pp. 351–382; R. Rosenthal, "Science and Ethics in Conducting, Analyzing, and Reporting Psychological Research," *Psychological Science*, 1994, vol. 5, pp. 127–134; R. Rosenthal and R. L. Rosnow, *The Volunteer Subject* (New York: Wiley); Rosnow, *Paradigms in Transition*, op. cit.

6. T. Mann, "Informed Consent for Psychological Research: Do Subjects Comprehend Consent Forms and Understand Their Legal Rights?" *Psychological Science*, 1994, vol. 5, pp. 140–143.

7. See, e.g., J. G. Adair, *The Human Subject: The Social Psychology of the Psychological Experiment* (Boston: Little, Brown, 1973); Campbell, "Prospective," op. cit.; G. T. Gardner, "Effects of Federal Human Subject Regulations on Data Obtained in Environmental Stressor Research," *Journal of Personality and Social Psychology*, 1978, vol. 36, pp. 628–634; G. Gniech, *Störeffekte in psychologischen Experimenten* (Stuttgart: Verlag W. Kohlhammer, 1976); J. Jung, *The Experimenter's Dilemma* (New York: Harper & Row, 1971); J. H. Resnick and T. Schwartz, "Ethical Standards as an Independent Variable in Psychological Research," *American Psychologist*, 1973, vol. 28, pp. 134–139; Rosenthal and Rosnow, *The Volunteer Subject*, op. cit.; Rosnow, *Paradigms in Transition*, op. cit.; H. Schuler, *Ethische Probleme psychologischer Forschung* (Göttingen: Verlag für Psychologie, 1980); I. Silverman, *The Human Subject in the Psychological Laboratory* (New York: Pergamon, 1977); J. M. Suls and R. L. Rosnow, "The Delicate Balance between Ethics and Artifacts in Behavioral Research," in A. J. Kimmel (Ed.), *New Directions for Methodology of Social and Behavioral Science: Ethics of Human Subject Research* (San Francisco: Jossey-Bass, 1981), pp. 55–67.

8. Resnick and Schwartz, "Ethical Standards as an Independent Variable in Psychological Research," op. cit.

9. The procedure was developed by C. Taffel, "Anxiety and the Conditioning of Verbal Behavior," *Journal of Abnormal and Social Psychology*, 1955, vol. 51, pp. 496–501.

10. Quoted from p. 138 in Resnick and Schwartz, "Ethical Standards as an Independent Variable in Psychological Research," op. cit.

11. Ibid.

12. Ibid.

13. Gardner, "Effects of Federal Human Subject Regulations on Data Obtained in Environmental Stressor Research," op. cit.

14. D. C. Glass and J. F. Singer, *Urban Stress: Experiments on Noise and Social Stressors* (New York: Academic Press, 1972).

15. Gardner, op. cit., p. 633.

16. See, for example, H. C. Kelman, "Human Use of Human Subjects: The Problem of Deception in Social Psychological Experiments," *Psychological Bulletin*, 1967, vol. 67, pp. 1–11; H. C. Kelman, *A Time to Speak: On Human Values and Social Research* (San Francisco: Jossey-Bass, 1968); M. B. Smith, "Conflicting Values Affecting Behavioral Research with Children," *Children*, 1967, vol. 14, pp. 53–58; M. B. Smith, *Social Psychology and Human Values* (Chicago: Aldine, 1969).

17. S. M. Jourard, "Experimenter-Subject Dialogue: A Paradigm for a Humanistic Science of Psychology," in J. F. T. Bugental (Ed.), *Challenges of Humanistic Psychology* (New York: McGraw-Hill, 1967), pp. 109–133; S. M. Jourard, *Disclosing Man to Himself* (New York: Van Nostrand Reinhold, 1968).

18. See, e.g., Kelman, "Human Use of Human Subjects," op. cit.; Kelman, *A Time to Speak*, op. cit.; H. C. Kelman, "The Rights of the Subject in Social Research: An Analysis in Terms of Relative Power and Legitimacy," *American Psychologist*, 1972, vol. 27, pp. 989–1016; H. C. Kelman, "Privacy and Research with Human Beings," *Journal of Social Issues*, 1977, vol. 33, pp. 169–195.

19. Kelman, *A Time to Speak*, op. cit., p. 211.

20. S. E. Asch, "Effects of Group Pressure upon the Modification and Distortion of Judgments," in G. E. Swanson, T. M. Newcomb, and E. L. Hartley (Eds.), *Readings in Social Psychology*, rev. ed. (New York: Holt, Rinehart & Winston, 1952), pp. 393–401.

21. For retrospectus, see S. Milgram, *Obedience to Authority* (New York: Harper Colophon, 1975); A. G. Miller, *The Obedience Experiments: A Case Study of Controversy in Social Science* (New York: Praeger, 1986).

22. L. J. Stricker, "The True Deceiver," *Psychological Bulletin*, 1967, vol. 68, pp. 13–20.

23. R. J. Menges, "Openness and Honesty Versus Coercion and Deception in Psychological Research," *American Psychologist*, 1973, vol. 28, pp. 1030–1034.

24. Quoted from p. 580 in R. Brown, *Social Psychology* (New York: Free Press, 1965).

25. I. Silverman, A. D. Shulman, and D. L. Wiesenthal, "Effects of Deceiving and Debriefing Psychological Subjects on Performance in Later Experiments," *Journal of Personality and Social Psychology*, 1970, vol. 14, pp. 203–212.

26. See H. K. Beecher, "Documenting the Abuses," *Saturday Review,* July 2, 1966, pp. 45–46; H. K. Beecher, *Research and the Individual: Human Studies* (Boston: Little, Brown, 1970).

27. See L. Humphreys, "New Styles in Homosexual Manliness," *Trans-Action,* 1971, vol. 8, pp. 38–46; L. Humphreys, *Tearoom Trade: Impersonal Sex in Public Places,* 2nd ed. (Chicago: Aldine, 1975).

28. Kelman, *A Time to Speak,* op. cit.

29. J. M. Darley, "The Importance of Being Earnest—and Ethical," *Contemporary Psychology,* 1980, vol. 25, pp. 563–611.

30. Ibid.

31. Smith, "Conflicting Values Affecting Behavioral Research with Children," op. cit.

32. S. W. Cook, G. A. Kimble, L. H. Hicks, W. J. McGuire, P. H. Schoggen, and M. B. Smith, "Ethical Standards for Psychological Research: Proposed Ethical Principles Submitted to the APA Membership for Criticism and Modification (by the) Ad Hoc Committee on Ethical Standards in Psychological Research," *APA Monitor,* 1971, vol. 2, no. 7, pp. 9–28.

33. S. W. Cook, L. H. Hicks, G. A. Kimble, W. J. McGuire, P. H. Schoggen, and M. B. Smith, "Ethical Standards for Research with Human Subjects," *APA Monitor,* 1972, vol. 3, no. 5, pp. I–XIX.

34. American Psychological Association, *Ethical Principles in the Conduct of Research with Human Participants* (Washington, DC: Author, 1982).

35. F. J. Arellano-Galdames, *Some Ethical Problems in Research on Human Subjects,* doctoral dissertation, University of New Mexico, Albuquerque, 1972.

36. See detailed discussion by B. Harris, "Key Words: A History of Debriefing in Social Psychology," in J. Morawski (Ed.), *The Rise of Experimentation in American Psychology* (New York: Oxford University Press, 1988), pp. 188–212.

37. Quote from E. B. Gurman, "Debriefing for All Concerned: Ethical Treatment of Human Subjects." *Psychological Science,* 1994, vol. 5, p. 139.

38. This idea was proposed by E. E. Jones and H. B. Gerard, *Foundations of Social Psychology* (New York: Wiley, 1967).

39. Blanck et al., "Scientific Rewards and Conflicts of Ethical Choices in Human Subjects Research," op. cit.

40. Ibid.

41. See H. Schuler, *Ethical Problems in Psychological Research* (New York: Acdaemic Press, 1982); originally published as Schuler, *Ethische Probleme psychologischer Forschung*, op. cit.

42. See also S. Bok's *Lying: Moral Choice in Public and Private Life* (New York: Pantheon, 1978).

43. J. L. Esposito, E. Agard, and R. L. Rosnow, "Can Confidentiality Pay Off?" *Personality and Individual Differences*, 1984, vol. 5, pp. 477–480.

44. S. J. Ceci and D. Peters, "Letters of Reference: A Naturalistic Study of the Effects of Confidentiality," *American Psychologist*, 1984, vol. 39, pp. 29–31.

45. For further discussion, see Blanck et al., "Scientific Rewards and Conflicts of Ethical Choices in Human Subjects Research," op. cit.

46. Cook et al., "Ethical Standards for Psychological Research," op. cit.

47. Quoted from p. 138 in Resnick and Schwartz, "Ethical Standards as an Independent Variable in Psychological Research," op. cit.

48. Quoted from p. 908 in K. J. Gergen, "Codification of Research Ethics: Views of a Doubting Thomas," *American Psychologist*, 1973, vol. 28, pp. 907–912.

49. D. S. Sullivan and T. E. Deiker, "Subject-Experimenter Perceptions of Ethical Issues in Human Research," *American Psychologist*, 1973, vol. 28, pp. 587–591.

50. S. Milgram, "Issues in the Study of Obedience: A Reply to Baumrind," *American Psychologist*, 1964, vol. 19, pp. 848–852.

51. See, e.g., D. Scott-Jones and R. L. Rosnow, "Ethics and Mental Health Research," in H. Freedman (Ed.), *Encyclopedia of Mental Health* (San Diego: Academic Press, in press).

52. Rosnow et al., "The Institutional Review Board as a Mirror of Scientific and Ethical Standards," op. cit.

53. Ibid.

54. Ibid.

55. See, e.g., discussion by S. J. Ceci, D. Peters, and J. Plotkin, "Human Subjects Review, Personal Values, and the Regulation of Social Science Research," *American Psychologist*, 1985, vol. 40, pp. 994–1002; P. C. Williams, "Success in Spite of Failure: Why IRBs Falter in Reviewing Risks and Benefits," *IRB: A Review of Human Subjects Research*, 1984, vol. 6, no. 3, pp. 1–4.

56. A. J. Kimmel, "Predictable Biases in the Ethical Decision Making of American Psychologists," *American Psychologist*, 1981, vol. 46, pp. 786–788.

57. See discussion in Rosenthal, "Science and Ethics in Conducting, Analyzing, and Reporting Psychological Research," op. cit.; R. Rosenthal, "Ethical Issues in Psychological Science: Risks, Consent, and Scientific Quality," *Psychological Science*, 1995, vol. 6, pp. 322–323; R. Rosenthal and R. L. Rosnow, "Applying Hamlet's Question to the Ethical Conduct of Research: A Conceptual Addendum," *American Psychologist*, 1984, vol. 39, pp. 561–563; R. Rosenthal and R. L. Rosnow, *Essentials of Behavioral Research: Methods and Data Analysis*, 2nd ed. (New York: McGraw-Hill, 1991); R. L. Rosnow, "Teaching Research Ethics through Role-play and Discussion," *Teaching of Psychology*, 1990, vol. 17, pp. 179–181; R. L. Rosnow and R. Rosenthal, *Beginning Behavioral Research: A Conceptual Primer*, 2nd ed. (Englewood Cliffs, NJ: Prentice-Hall, 1996).

58. Quoted from p. 839 in J. Kaplan, "The Use of Animals in Research," *Science*, 1988, vol. 242, pp. 839–840.

59. See Rosenthal, "Science and Ethics in Conducting, Analyzing, and Reporting Psychological Research," op. cit.

60. Quoted from p. 89 in J. Atwell, "Human Rights in Human Subjects Research," in A. J. Kimmel (Ed.), *New Directions for Methodology of Social and Behavioral Science: Ethics of Human Subject Research* (San Francisco: Jossey-Bass, 1981), pp. 81–90.

61. For detailed discussions of these and other issues in the ethics of research in the behavioral and social sciences, see Rosenthal, "Science and Ethics in Conducting, Analyzing, and Reporting Psychological Research," op. cit.; J. E. Sieber (Ed.), *The Ethics of Social Research: Fieldwork, Regulation, and Publication* (New York: Springer-Verlag, 1981); J. E. Sieber (Ed.), *The Ethics of Social Research: Surveys and Experiments* (New York: Springer-Verlag, 1982).

62. I. Berlin, *The Hedgehog and the Fox: An Essay on Tolstoy's View of History* (New York: Simon & Schuster, 1953).

63. G. Holton, "From the Endless Frontier to the Ideology of Limits," in G. Holton and R. S. Morison (Eds.), *Limits of Scientific Inquiry* (New York: Norton, 1978), pp. 227–241.

64. Ibid.

Name Index

Subject Index

About the Authors

Ralph L. Rosnow and Robert Rosenthal are both well known for their scholarly work in the area of research methodology, and they have written many books together, including the successful textbooks *Essentials of Behavioral Research* and *Beginning Behavioral Research*. Rosnow, who also coauthored *Writing Papers in Psychology*, received his Ph.D. from American University and is the Thaddeus Bolton Professor of Psychology at Temple University. Rosenthal received his Ph.D. from UCLA and is now the Edgar Pierce Professor of Psychology at Harvard University.